Has All Been Said

HAS ALL BEEN SAID

The collected works of
Sibyl Croly Hanchett Schneller

Compiled and edited by
Marie Chandler Gale

HAS ALL BEEN SAID

Publisher: Cinnabar Press
            www.cinnabar-press.com

Copyright © 2019 by Marie C. Gale. All Rights Reserved.

Cover art copyright @ 2019 Roxanne Fawcett. All Rights Reserved.

Individual poems copyright the estate, heirs and assigns of Sibyl Schneller.

Photographs are from photo collections of Sibyl Schneller and her descendants, and to the best of our knowledge are copyright the estate, heirs and assigns of Sibyl Schneller.

No part of this book may be reproduced or transmitted in any form by any means, electronic, mechanical, photocopy, recording or otherwise without the prior written permission of the publisher. For information on getting permission for reprints and excerpts, contact the publisher at info@cinnabar-press.com.

ISBN 978-0-9795945-7-1

Paradox

I discovered to my surprise
that I am like everyone else.
Later I discovered,
still to my surprise,
that everyone else
is not like me.

– Sibyl (Croly) (Hanchett) Schneller

TABLE OF CONTENTS

Paradox......................................v
Preface xv
Sibyl's Story 1
Birth & Youth 13
    For Happiness...........................15
    Kind Souls 15
    Birth and the Pursuit of Happiness 16
    Shh!...................................17
    Too Short a Dream 18
    Quiet Repose 18
    To a Fair Lad 19
    Youth 20
    Young Feet.............................20
    Friends................................21
    Realism 22
    Dream Children 24
    I See a Boy............................25

Table of Contents

Romance, Love & Love Lost 27

- A Small Adventure 29
- Always 30
- Looking Back. 30
- You Could Manage a Star 31
- Nor the Alternative 31
- Only With Music. 32
- Thirty Seven to Seventeen 33
- Poet Lovers 34
- The Eternal Joy 35
- Ordeal at Dawn 36
- The Machine Age 37
- Knight Errant. 38
- Moonin' 41
- Almost a Memory 42
- Moon Driven 43
- New Year's Eve of 1905 44
- The Man in the Moon. 46
- A Whimper 47
- Inconsistency. 48
- To a Greek Head 49
- Two Loves 50
- Unexpressed 52
- Dark Water 53
- No Candle Burning. 53
- Shopworn 54
- I Warn You. 54
- A Song 55
- Aftermath 56
- Exit Line. 56

Chess or Contract 57
Incomplete. 58

People. 59

Herself. 61
Her Picture 62
Empty Chairs. 62
A Simple Man 63
Martyr Complex. 64
Is That So 64
To A.J.C.. 65
The Office Secretary 66
To Art Eisler. 66
To M.D. 67
The Poet. 67
To Sara Teasdale 68
Marc. 69
Privacy Achieved 70
Home-Coming. 71
Rude Words. 71
Grandma Eschews Parsley 72
New England Ancestry 72
My Education (Hieronymus Bosch) 73
Place Names of Marin. 74
Mill Valley to Malibu. 75
Why Bother 76
Merry Christmas - Happy New Year. 76

Regret, Pain & Sorrow. 77

Unfinished Story. 79

Table of Contents

Hokku of Expectancy 80
Hokku of Happiness 80
Hokku for Tears 81
Hokku of Pain 81
Dawn Stirrings 82
Has All Been Said 83
A Happy Thought 84
Airless Night 84
Dream 85
The Bell Team 86

Political Commentary 87

1940 89
Berry Hill 90
Good News on the Radio 91
Schweitzer 92
Resistance 93
New Orleans, 1960 93
Unfit 94
He Stirreth Up the People 96
Whither From Earth 97
The Piano 98
Fate and Love 100
From California 101

Philosophical Reflections 103

Too Late Smart 105
The Philosopher 105
Tell the World 105
A Square Inch of Space 106
The Crusade Spirit 107

Pastime 107
Terrible Words. 107
Truth 108
A Small Song. 108
Fugue by Wilhelm Friedmann Bach 109
An Article of Furniture 110
My Pearls. 112
(An Answer) 114
Kings 1:1-4 116
Forbidden Fruit 118
Wholesome Fun 118
Babel 119
A Sower 120

Plants, Animals & Nature 121

The Ginkgo Tree 123
Survival 123
In a Garden 124
Fern Fingers 124
Antaeus 125
Green Things 125
Dryads 126
Dryads Curious 127
To the Father Tree. 128
The Caterpillar 128
The Civilized Rabbit 129
After a Thousand Years. 130
Freedom. 130
Cat in the Old Village Grocery 131
Spring Scenario. 131

Table of Contents

    Felines 132

    Old Friends 133

    I Hate Dogs 134

    California Summer Song 135

    From a Car Window 135

    The Suppliant 136

    Ants 136

    Self-Restraint in April 137

    Dust Thou Art 138

    Prelude 139

    La Noche 140

    An Unusual Honor 141

    Unfriendly Skies 141

Mock Us Gently 143

    Mock Us Gently 145

    Overheard 145

    Flattery Will Get You 146

    One of Life's Moments 147

    Two Big Words 148

    Our Grandchildren 148

    You and I Were Young, Maggie 149

    The Wheel Chair 149

    One Answer 150

    I Was Privileged 151

    Fondly Remembered 152

    Channel 5 152

    Music Critic 153

    The Whisper 153

    Don't Feed the Pigeons 154

Dialog with a Strawberry 154
Incident in a Low Key. 155
The Sinner. 155
Violet 156
Call Me Buck 157
We Entertained Royalty. 158

Aging, Death & God 159

Vision Before Choice 161
Squandered 162
Silence. 162
Immortality 163
Apropos of Roses. 164
When One Book Closes 164
A Prayer. 165
Cameos 165
Old Rose 166
The Body Speaks. 167
I Am What I Am When I Am. 167
My Town 168
If I Will 168
Houses. 169
A Long View 170
As It Might Happen 171
Moving Day (Inventory) 174
Bronze Chrysanthemums. 175
A Hope. 176
Heaven. 177
The Teacher. 178
Departure. 178

Table of Contents

Humor & Wordplay 179
Jealous Doggy-Rel 181
Short Story 181
Jymn's Hymn 181
Stately Names of England 182
Re-Verse 184
Young Hero 184
Pippa Passes 185
Surrealist Trilogy 186
The Fur Cup 186
The Fur Saucer 187
The Fur Spoon 188
Geography and Poetry 189
Valentine Verses 190

Women of the Bible 193
The Story of Cain as Told By His Wife 195
Sons of Eve 201
Daughter of Lot 205
Sarah 211
Rebekah 217
Leah 223
David's First Wife 231
Naomi the Weaver 239

Appendix - Interesting Facts 243

Index 253

PREFACE

As one of Sibyl's eleven grandchildren, I received copies of both her poetry books — *A Square Inch of Space* in 1974 and *Mock Us Gently* in 1978. They sat on the shelf and I felt a glowing pride in my heritage when I looked at them. However, I am sorry to admit that I never really took the time to carefully read the poems and understand what she had to say.

It wasn't until I started sorting and organizing the materials in our "Family Archive" that I realized what an excellent and prolific poet Grandma Sibyl really was. She wrote poetry from age 7 to just prior to her death at age 94. She had poetry published in books, magazines and newspapers, and won several poetry competitions.

My first find consisted of the poems that she apparently collected and retyped at some point in her later life. Between the materials I received from her, my mother and my Aunt Hilda's estate, I had literally hundreds of slips of paper with poems on them.

After a thorough review and comparison of the contents of *A Square Inch of Space*, *Mock Us Gently*, and the loose poems, I thought I had at last found all of Sibyl's poetry. Boy, was I wrong!

Sibyl's father recorded her very first poem, written at age 7, in her Baby Book. Later, Sibyl apparently used the back half of the book as a journal of sorts, and it contained a number of poems and short stories she wrote. That poetry was added to this collection.

Preface

Included in the collection of papers and books I received from Sibyl was a book of poetry, *A Day in the Hills*, published in 1926. On a hunch, I checked and found it contained a selection of poems from a poetry competition — which Sibyl won. Of the five of Sibyl's poems included in the book, three were ones I hadn't seen before. They, too, were added to the collection.

Finally, when researching the publication dates of some of the poems, I found yet another poem I had not seen before. It was added to the collection, bringing the total number of Sibyl's poems to an even 200.

Over half of the poems I've located are unpublished; many of the published poems are in books, magazines and newspapers that are no longer easily accessible. Not one living person besides me had ever seen a majority of Sibyl's poems. While the world at large may or may not be interested in her poetry and the understanding of her life that comes from reading it, I felt I owed it to her family to at least make it possible for them to read her works. And so this book was conceived.

I am not absolutely certain that I've found every single one of her poems—but I believe this is most of them. Based on a few comments Sibyl made in her other writing, she entered some poetry competitions in the first half of the 20th Century, for which there may have been books or magazines published containing the competing poems. So far, all of these have eluded my search.

The layout of the book and the organization of the poems is completely my handiwork, with the exception of the content of the chapters "Mock Us Gently" which contains all the poems from the book of that title, and "Women of the Bible" which contains the poems Sibyl submitted for a new book. Choosing how to group the poems, and interpreting which chapter a poem should be placed in was a difficult task. I hope no one is too offended by my choices.

Material for Chapter 1, "Sibyl's Story," was compiled from a wide array of sources, most of which are included in our "Family Archive." I am very thankful that Sibyl wrote not only poetry, but also short stories and essays, many of which were clearly about her life as a child and young woman. She was also quite outspoken and well-regarded in her community, which resulted in numerous magazine and newspaper articles about her activities and accomplishments.

Finally, the appendix contains whatever interesting tidbits I found out about each of the poems in this book, which in some cases may help to give insight into the context of the poem. The appendix notes whether or not a poem was published (to the best of my knowledge), and includes the date(s) and place(s) of publication, if known.

To my nieces, nephews and cousins — Sibyl's more than 60 descendants — this book is for you. I hope you take the time to read it and that doing so gives you an insight into the life, loves, losses, likes, and dislikes of your ancestress and a better understanding of who that amazing woman was.

Marie (Chandler) Gale
February, 2019

Note: More information about Sibyl and her life can be found at www.lookingupthedust.com.

1

SIBYL'S STORY

Sibyl Mary Croly was born on Leap Year Day (February 29th), 1888 in Cadillac, Michigan, the daughter of James Croly (born December, 1838 in Canada) and Maria Amelia (Cowles) Dennett (born January 1st, 1944 in Ohio).

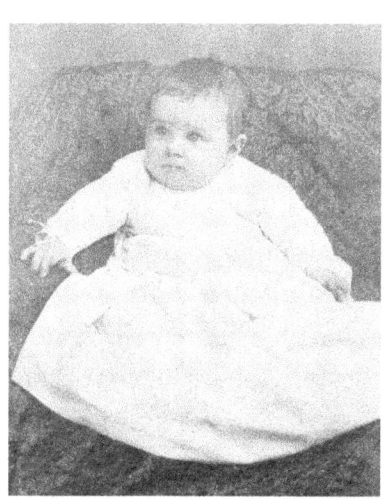

Sibyl's first picture, ca. summer 1888

James was the son of Irish immigrants who arrived in Canada around 1800. Maria, on the other hand, was the great-granddaughter of Revolutionary War hero, Colonel Alexander Harper, and a descendant of James Harper, a Scots-Irish immigrant who arrived in America in 1720. According to family tradition, James didn't know that Maria was Irish and was intimidated by her long history in America.

Sibyl's Story

James and Maria were married in December, 1875. James was 37 when they married; Maria was 31. Both had been married previously and had older children from their first marriages. James' son, Charles, was born in 1868, and Maria's daughter, Mary Irene, was born in 1877.

Sibyl, age 19 months

Sibyl's parents had been married for 13 years when she was born. Her father was 50 and her mother was 44. By 1888 standards, they were both well beyond the years to expect the arrival of a new baby. For her parents, Sibyl was a late-life miracle and a joy in their lives. They doted on her. Her father summed it up in his entry in her baby journal in December, 1890:

I have been very busy this summer and have been away from home most of the time, and have seen very little of my darling. How she has grown into my heart; how she has become so much a part of my life; how much her sweet personality pervades all my thought, I cannot tell here. Once in a great while, I try with a full heart and streaming eyes to speak of my love to the mother, so that she understands, but how we love each other and how we both love the baby is something akin to our love for Christ, too sacred to talk about.

Both Sibyl's parents were avid readers (her father was an editor at one point), and she was imbued with a love of reading and words at an early age. Creative writing followed naturally. Her first published piece was a letter to Santa submitted to a local contest, for which she won first place in the class for children between 6 and 8 years old (she was 5 1/2).

Sibyl attended kindergarten in Michigan. The following summer, the family moved to an 80-acre vineyard outside Lincoln, California. According to Sibyl, it was "miles from other children." The fact of living amongst adults, who themselves both read and wrote prolifically, likely influenced both the quantity and quality of her writing.

Her first poem, ("Quiet Repose" on page 16) was written at the age of seven for her sister who was getting married. One expects that she may have been known for her writing and/or poetry even in grammar school. Her poem "Geography and Poetry" (page 179) which was co-authored with another 6th grade student at age 11, was published in the local paper and at least one year she ghost wrote several Valentine's day poems in the names of other students (page 180).

Sibyl, 1906
(probably High School Graduation picture)

Sibyl the Romantic, 1907

In 1903, at the age of 15, Sibyl moved with her family to San Jose, where she finished high school. The book that started as her Baby Journal, written by her father, morphed into a composition book containing essays, poems and short stories written during her adolescent years (probably both before and after completing high school).

Sibyl graduated from San Jose High School in 1906, just several weeks after the Great San Francisco earthquake wreaked havoc with the high school building. The following fall, she attended San Jose Normal (now San Jose State University), from which she graduated in 1909 with a major in education and minors in music and English.

The following school year (1909-10) found Sibyl teaching in a small school in Lake County, California. That summer Sibyl returned to San Jose and married Lorraine Joseph Hanchett in San Jose, California. The when and how of their romance remains a mystery, as does their exact marriage date and place.

Lorraine (commonly called "LJ") was born June 26, 1888, in San Jose California, son of Joseph Edward Hanchett (born in Wisconsin in 1845) and Mary Josephine Nelson (born about 1858 in California).

Sibyl and LJ lived in the San Jose area – mostly in Saratoga – during their marriage. LJ was working as an Assistant Superintendent of the Street Railway in 1910, as an accountant for a cannery in 1920 and then as the Vice President of Sales for the Cannery in 1930. During their marriage they had five children, four of whom lived to adulthood:

i. Barbara Josephine, born 6 April 1911, died 1978, married Charles W. Chandler in 1932.

ii. Edward Lorraine, born 4 July 1912, died 1966, married first Clara Waldo, second Pearl Yee.

iii. William Verne, born 26 September 1914, died 1944, married first, Fran, and second, Marion Brimer Baron.

iv. Alfred Robert, Born 18 March 1918, died 24 June 1918.

v. Hilda Madeline, born 27 February 1920, died 2007, married first James Hulquist and second Paul Fourman.

The death of Alfred Robert at just 3 months of age had a profound impact on Sibyl. Not only was there the devastating loss of a child, that loss was compounded by the fact that Alfred apparently died of polio and Sibyl was told he contracted it because she was a carrier without symptoms. That loss and despair can be seen in a number of her poems.

Sibyl with children, ca. 1923
(l to r: Sibyl, Hilda, Edward (Ned), Honey (a cousin), Barbara, and Billy)

By around 1923, Sibyl was teaching in the music education and piano departments of San Jose State. She taught music there for 17 years. She continued to teach piano until well into her 80's. About her career, in 1931 she wrote in "A Letter to My Great-Grandchildren":

> *Perhaps I should mention that I teach piano at the State College in San Jose. The wage — or salary — earning mothers, I understand, are getting to be a problem, social and economic. I am sorry to add to the complications of society, but it seems to work out fairly well in this case, though I admit the case is an exception. My work has been of a sort which would bear the interruption of small children, and it has taken me with them into school, rather than away from them. Anyhow, I am a very casual housekeeper and a fairly earnest teacher — I am probably happier this way.*

Sibyl, ca. 1930

Throughout her time teaching and raising children, Sibyl continued to write. Her body of work included essays, stories, a published novel (*Late Harvest*, published in 1937), songs, several anthems and short piano pieces, a children's operetta, a music textbook, and a myriad of poetry. Sibyl apparently didn't keep copies of the music compositions, textbook or operetta[1] but, thankfully, she was relatively diligent about keeping copies of her poetry.

Sibyl had a strong romantic streak with infatuations, crushes and several affairs from adolescence until well into her later years. These emotional roller-coasters of the heart are strongly evidenced in many of her poems — so many, in fact, that in this book a whole chapter is devoted to them.)

In addition to her writing and teaching, Sibyl was an avid needlepointer. Her tapestries, most of which she designed herself, graced her home. Many of her tapestries can be found in the homes of her descendants today. About her living room in 1931 she said:

I have arranged this particular shelf together with a blue vase which stands on top, with a needlepoint tapestry in predominating blues which hangs above. The vase will hardly survive to your day, short of a miracle, but a poor old faded tapestry may be intact. I made it about four years ago and the colors are more vigorous now than they will be after half a century of sunlight.

---

[1] Copies of the operetta and textbook have not yet been located, but the search is ongoing.

There is another tapestry, which will probably be less durable, in silk. I have another wool one started, but they take a lot of eyesight, and either energy or leisure, so it is in obeisance[2] until I am less actively employed than at present.

Further descriptions of her home in 1931 give evidence to the interconnectedness of her love of both needlepoint and poetry:

... on the wall above is an embroidered picture which is perhaps not very artistic, but I had a good deal of fun doing it, and it inspired a set of seven poems called "Tapestry". These poems swelled appreciatively the volume of your ancestress's published works[3].

Sibyl, ca. 1955

In 1938, with all her children grown and married, Sibyl spent several weeks in Reno, Nevada, coming home with a final divorce decree ending her marriage to LJ. Two months later, LJ had remarried and by 1940 he was living in Seattle, Washington. By 1941, Sibyl was married to Marcus Schneller, a brewer with Pacific Brewing Company, and living in Saratoga.

Marcus Schneller died in 1947, leaving Sibyl a widow and on her own. Shortly thereafter,

---

2 obeisance: acknowledgment of another's superiority or importance. Sibyl may have used this word as a play on "abeyance," which is defined as a state of temporary disuse or suspension.

3 The "set of seven poems" as originally published has not been located. They were likely the foundation of "A Square Inch of Space" (page 102) and "Knight Errant" (page 36), of which several versions have been found.

Sibyl's Story

Sibyl, ca. 1963, with her beloved grand piano, braille typewriter and her "Unicorn in Captivity" tapestry.

Sibyl moved to Mill Valley, California, where her three living adult children resided.

While no longer teaching music in a school setting, she continued to teach private students and played the organ every Sunday for the local Methodist church. All told, she actively taught music and/or piano, and played for her church and/or for entertainment for a continuous span of nearly 80 of her 96 years.

In the mid-1960's, Sibyl discovered that her sight was degenerating. Knowing she would need to rely on the Talking Book program of the Library of Congress for her reading material, Sibyl devised a way to "pay it forward" by transcribing written music scores into Braille. After completing the training classes, she was certified by the Library of Congress in both literary and music brailling in 1965. Over the next decade she dedicated many hours to transcribing hundreds (maybe even thousands) of pages of classical and contemporary music into Braille for the Library of Congress.

During her life, Sibyl also had a definite competitive streak. In 1889, at just 19 months, Sibyl won the Cadillac News and Express "Handsomest Baby" contest, and at 5½ she won the 1893 "letter to Santa" competition previously mentioned. In 1932, Sibyl tied for first place in the California State Spelling Bee for adult spellers, a feat of which she was quite proud. Her recipe for Date Cashew Honeys, entered into the 1955 Pillsbury Bake-Off, earned her a seat as one of the 100 finalists to travel to New York City for the official bake-off at the Waldorf–Astoria Hotel and a place in the 1956 recipe book as a Senior Winner in the cookie category. For her designed and executed petite-point tapestry based on "The Unicorn in Captivity," she entered — and won 2nd place — in the wall hanging class of the Tenth National Exhibition of the Amateur Needlework in New York City in 1957.

In addition to the competitions in various non-literary disciplines, throughout her life she entered her poetry into various competitions—and often won there as well. In 1926, she submitted a collection of poems to the annual poetry competition of the Edwin Markham Chapter of the English Poetry Society of the Teacher's College in San Jose. She won first place with her poem "Home-Coming" (page 71) and it was published along with several other of her poems in *A Day in the Hills*, a small volume containing an anthology of selected poetry from the competition. According to her records, the poem, "As It Might Happen" (page 171) won "first place in a 1935 Los Angeles poetry contest."[4] Finally, at age 90, she entered her poem "Ordeal at Dawn" (page 36)into the Contra Costa (California) County Fair poetry competition — and won. Given her propensity to enter into contests and competitions and the volume and quality of her poetry, it is quite likely that there were entries submitted to many other poetry contests; what they were and whether she won, we'll probably never know.

Quite a few of her poems were also printed in local or regional newspapers and periodicals including the *Mu Phi Epsilon Triangle*, The *Saturday Review*, The *Santa Ana Register*, The *People's World*, The *Independent Journal* (Marin Country, CA), *Warp and Woof*, *American Lyric Poetry*, and others. Whether inclusion of her poetry in these publications was a result of some contest or whether she submitted them for

---

[4] The date and name of the contest have not yet been identified.

publication isn't known. Either way, she was certainly industrious about getting her poetry viewed and read.

In 1974, the first book of her poetry, *A Square Inch of Space,* was published with the assistance of her sorority, Mu Phi Epsilon. It contains a collection of 65 selected poems written over the course of her life. Following the success of her first publication, a second book of her poetry, *Mock Us Gently,* was published in 1974. It contains 21 poems, all of which were reflections upon life at The Redwoods, the retirement community to which Sibyl had moved in about 1970.

During her sunset years while residing at The Redwoods, Sibyl wrote a series of eight poems chronicling the lives of women of the Bible. Although she submitted to several publishers, it was never published.

Also during that time she spent time reflecting on her life. There is evidence that she reviewed her existing poetry, retyping and making minor edits to existing poems. She also wrote a number of new poems, many about incidents or people in her early life (some of which are even dated with the year the original incident took place).

Sibyl passed away at the home of her one living child, Hilda, on March 7, 1982, at age 94 — having just had her 23rd Leap Year Day birthday.

Throughout her life, she was ahead of her time. A working mother in the 1920's, a published novelist in the 1930's, a divorcée in the 40's, and a self-supporting widow in the 50's (and on), a poet and music teacher for her entire lifetime. The legacy she passed to her descendants and others is diverse and extensive, ranging from needlepoint tapestries and books of verse to the love of music and prose. She instilled in her children and grand-children a deep appreciation for family, personal self-reliance, and not falling prey to the societal "now you are supposed to" dictates which limited the women of her day.

And then, of course, there are those Date Pecan Honeys!

Sibyl Mary Croly, age 90 (1978)

2

BIRTH & YOUTH

For Happiness

Come into this world
born into a family
but seek your kindred

and having found them
let your heart, hands, brain and time
be at their service.

Kind Souls

Kind souls were waiting
when I arrived in this world;
they took care of me.
You talk about God;
you talk too much about god
and I am confused.
But I know kind souls;
I have been in their company.
Kind souls, care for me.

Birth and the Pursuit of Happiness

At first it seemed I had been sent to hell
for I was cut off from companionship
and cast out from the comfort I had known.
I fought for a strangling breath to send a cry
of terror into the vast unheeding space.

A hand, unrecognized but not unkind,
touched me and lifted me with the assurance
that I was not alone. I set myself
to breathe, to call aloud for food, to suck
and do the human things that must be done.

I learned I had been sent to Planet Earth,
otherwise known as purgatory, where
each living soul receives its own earned chance
to be content in its own kind of hell
or take a tremulous halting step toward heaven.

If you are granted many years on Earth,
accept the gift with grace; assimilate
experience. Digest the memories
that flood your nights and fertilize the soul
for future harvest. Count this time well spent.

When incidents of misplaced fortitude
present themselves, with debt of unshed tears,
do not refuse to weep; the shower dispels
the cloud, and you have need of clarity
and light upon the road that lies ahead.

Shh!

Surprisingly I find myself
among the grown-ups.
My head is as far from the floor as theirs,
I see I must be careful
of my behavior.

You also are tall,
but I suspect you.
Sometimes you are too quiet,
and I have heard you tell the truth
unnecessarily.
Be warned,
for I have thought this matter out.
Some of these people are really grown up!

Too Short a Dream

My father milked the cow by lantern light;
I stood in the shadowy barn, my pony came
and laid a friendly head against my shoulder.
I patted her, and when I left the barn
my dog went running with me toward the house.

This was the whole dream, a scene, a touch
of living memory from a distant past,
and all that day I felt I had been blest,
but I'd have loved to reach the kitchen door
and hear my mother say, "Come set the table."

Quiet Repose

Safe in the cradle of the tree,
Sleeps the birdie that sings;
Safe in the rose's pink curtained rooms,
Sleeps the elf that has wings.

Safe in the ground the acorn is,
Which sometime will be a tree;
Safe, all tucked in bed I am,
While Christ is watching o'er me.

So everything is safe, in the care
of Him that died,
So many the time that man
has sinned;
Christ, the Lord has sighed.

To a Fair Lad

How youth must suffer being young!
How the impatient soul resents
The fair, smooth cheek, the unskilled tongue,
The chrysalid of innocence,
The form in which he walks encased,
The slow unfolding toward release,
While hounds of all a world in haste
Snap at his nerves and rend his peace.

Will you, as others, trade the sting
And eagerness that drives you now
For ease, for love, for anything?
Come back in ten years; tell me how
The light falls on your landscape then;
Whether your life elects to be
Successful with the sorry men
Or brave, in better company.

Chrysalid: *Synonym for chrysalis. In the pupa of a butterfly, it is the form of the insect when it is between the larval and adult stages in a case or cocoon.*

Youth

Youth passes. Let it pass. Who will regret it?
I speak the truth, for pastime, say it is
a span of anguish so incredible
that few who have survived it will admit
the memory. Hence a well-constructed myth
extols its roseate dreams and golden joys.
This would not in itself be very harmful
except for sorry children who may hear
and wonder what undreamed-of sadnesses
make youth seem happy by comparison.

Young Feet

There is a path that cuts the college lawn
Across a corner or two, ignores, derides
The obese concrete curve prescribed by law.
No more than eighteen inches wide, enough
For walking, not to trample growing things
For wantonness. An arrogant little path,
Slender, direct, indomitable. Bars
Are sometimes placed across, and it defers
To them, and spoils the minimum of grass
In a semicircular detour, and goes on.

Deride: *to laugh at in contempt or scorn; make fun of; ridicule.*

Friends

A dusty heap of shabby books
    In the attic corner lies,
And I found them waiting there patiently,
    Forgotten by loving eyes.

There are dear old volumes of childish days,
    Some stained with childish tears,
And some are dog's-eared, and some are torn,
    And all show the trace of years.

A shabby copy of "Undine" lies
    Next the "Arabian Nights",
And the torn "Swiss Family Robinson" brings
    A thrill of the old delights.

There's "Five Little Peppers" (they've since grown up)
    And "Anderson's Fairy Tales," too,
Bring memories of the bygone days
    When fairy tales were true.

New friends may come and friends may go,
    And loves may flourish and die,
But up in the attic the old books wait
    With the comfort of days gone by.

Realism

I was a little child at play
    And vivid fancy oft would bring
Glimpses of pixie, elf, or fay,
    More real than mere imagining;
They came to sorrow or rejoice,
    'Neath leaden clouds or skies of blue,
But with them an insistent voice
    Murmured, "No fairy tales are true."

I had a playhouse built for me,
    My childish treasures there I brought,
Flowers, dolls and books in loving glee,
    To tempt the fairies was my thought;
Sometimes I fancied they were near
    And would their airy forms pursue,
Trying to turn unheeding ear
    To that which breathed, "It is not true."

When older I would turn my eyes
    Away from daily pressing care,
To where a world of sunshine lies
    Which only conscious dreamers share.
And there the fairies took my hand,
    We trod those pleasant gardens through --
If truth shuts me from fairyland
    Then I would cling to dreams untrue.

Yet older now-- the years have passed
    And crowded out those early dreams
And they have taught my heart at last
    "What is" is rather than "what seems."
We need not search in fairy lore,
    Nor wander pleasant gardens through
To find the key to heaven's door
    The best of fairy tales is true.

Dream Children

I was a solitary child,
My playmates phantom children wild,
My foes their aunts sour and old
With whetted tongue made sharp to scold.

One dear decade of childhood glee
My little air friends dwelt with me,
But as these shortening years roll on,
I feel with sorrow they are gone.

They viewed life's vistas long and fair,
But knew they might not enter there.
They saw the new loves coming fast,
But their place is the dear dim past.

At the dark close of a lost day
They came to me in sad array.
The long procession then began
with "Dream Girl," "Clara," "Chocolate Man."

And others came with wistful eye,
Their time had come to say good-bye.
Dear wee "Rentina" whom I loved
More than the others, sadly moved.

And as they went two warm tears fell
My little childish dreams -- Farewell.

I See a Boy

I see a boy with nervous, gentle face,
Reedy and awkward, spectacled and slim,
Unconfident of what life holds for him,
What his appointed work and where his place;
Searching the wilderness for a guiding trace;
Eyes keen for colors yet far-off and dim;
Ears tuned to harmonies of the seraphim;
Hands slender, agile, meet for art and grace.

To this disturbed earth, whose brutal need
Must over-ride his fineness and his power,
Why, at this moment, did he choose to come
Seeking the climate to mature his seed?
In this confused and fratricidal hour
Where on this planet can he be at home?

Seraphim: *Angels who are forever in God's presence, "Day and night without ceasing they sing: 'Holy, holy holy is the Lord God Almighty, who was and is and is to come." (quoting book of Revelation (iv 4-8)*

3

ROMANCE, LOVE & LOVE LOST

A Small Adventure

A lover and his lady-might-have-been
Meet at a ball; they tread the minuet,
Galliard, waltz, two-step; slip into that net
Of intricate sweet sophisticated sin,
The tango. They embrace, they smile, forget
For a moment all the laughter, lights and din,
And mirror with their eyes those glades wherein
Down all the centuries, they have never met.

Light footed weaves the pattern of the dance,
With deft perfection of unconscious art.
His touch is wine to her adventurous heart;
He quaffs the heady nectar of her glance;
Her eyes to him, his hands to her, impart
The ecstasy of unfulfilled romance.

Galliard archaic: *a lively Renaissance dance in triple time for two people with intricate steps, popular in Europe during the 16th century.*

Always

Always, you said, I knew it could not be;
My lips refused all answer but a smile.
I, who had dealt with time a longer while;
Than you, had fathomed that word's falsity.
Then, one inevitable day, we knew:
You could not look into my eyes again
With pleading or with pleasure; I wore then
The same smile in commending you adieu.

Life's patchwork pattern misses, here and there,
The rare bright range of colors I could see
Only through your eyes: on deaf ears will fall
Unheeded, harmonies only you could share
And translate; your old word comes back to me,
For, always, where you were is emptiness.

Looking Back

One evening of an ordinary day,
Without complaint (the penalty was just)
I stood and watched as you rode away
Trailing my heart after you in the dust.

Looking back on that moment through the years,
The many years reaching from now to then,
I marvel, though that day was dry of tears,
How I survived to weep and laugh again.

You Could Manage a Star

If I threw a star to you
you would not let it burn your hands
nor would you let it fall at your feet,
wondering dumbly
why I was playing the fool
with a bit of glass.

You would catch it on your fingertips
and toss it back to be brighter.

Nor the Alternative

A thrifty, base advantage I must take;
Devour your love, and offer you a taste
Of half-love in exchange; no royal waste
Befits a balanced heart, too sane to break.
For I do not forget, not ever, quite,
That you may suddenly walk completely free
Of the frail gossamers that grapple me,
At any hour of any day or night.

When the awakening comes I would be there
to meet your new glance imperturbable,
And say, "Congratulations, friend!" that these
Cool words may prove me calm and debonair,
And the episode, for all concerned, end well.

Only With Music

Only with music can I share
your presence. I can bear
to be in your arms and feel a violin
thrusting its vibrance in
between us; or a flute
high, remote, acute
with spiritual portent, like a cry
out of infinity.

Love's quality belongs
to these; even old songs,
strung with word-tokens minted long ago
and thinned in petty trade, will throw
your glance flaming to mine,
and the old words shine
exquisite, freshly fair
for us, as for the lover who set them there.

Thirty Seven to Seventeen

He tells me you are only seventeen
And I believe it. I've been watching you
And caught youth's ancient trouble lurking through
Your pretty glitter. Furthermore, I've seen
You anxiously coquettish as you preen
Your silken plumage in my lover's view.

And he may kiss your tender lips, your eyes,
The smooth pink flesh that lures him on to love
Mirage, whatever it is a man does kiss;
Still I serene, controlled, or oddly wise
I cannot take you seriously enough
For jealousy, poor pitiful chrysalis.

Poet Lovers

We must not speak. Our talk must be of things
Casual, unimportant; we must not hear
The slow, insistent throbbing of muted strings
Between our hearts; we have so much to fear,
Knowing so much, exploring as we do
In twilight depths, to mint a sacred pain
Deftly into a facile line or two ...
Dare we be still and listen to the rain?

Dear, when this silence, love-encumbered, girds
Itself to utterance, hidden wish compressed
In beautiful, unnecessary words
Or rounded tear and facet-pointed jest;
Then we who share this aching stillness long
May know relieving rhapsodies of song.

The Eternal Joy

When in the trees the young white moon gleams crescent
Adown her fluid pathway of pure light
Fleet-footed Beauty, changeful, iridescent,
Eludes the mourning reaches of the night.
Ah, lovely, lonely wandering forest sprite,
Who, having visioned, can forbear to love thee?
Who, that has tasted once the deep delight
Of that pure passion, holds aught else above thee?

Let not my longing eyes to loitering move thee,
My pleading hands, nor eager wistful feet;
Draw close to the enchanted draperies moonlight wove thee;
Fling back a cadence of thy laughter sweet.
So shalt thou guide me in thy path pursuing,
Fresh in my soul the eternal joy of wooing.

Adown: *archaic: down or downward*
Aught: *anything whatever*

Ordeal at Dawn

Now dawn shall separate us who have lain
Intimately companioned through the night;
Who jointly have out-stared the arrogant white
Countenance of reality, to gain
A shared infliction of ecstatic pain;
And sinking, panic smitten, down the flight
Of swift insensate hours toward the light,
We striving to be one, must now be twain.

In that dim pool where all the senses blur
And mingle, that Lethean darkness where
The soul's uncertain boundaries melt away,
Submerged and blended, we have dared incur
This penalty. How much it was to dare
We shall not know until the stroke of day.

Lethean: *Causing oblivion or forgetfulness of the past. From the river Lethe in Hades, whose water when drunk made the souls of the dead forget their life on earth.*

The Machine Age

The crystal wash of rain has overlaid
The glass before us, and with hasty beat
Its small sky missiles tap their incomplete
Rhythm of their vagrant music overhead.
All moving lights are scattered and besprayed
Along the beetle surface of the street,
And every little flying world we meet
Appears mysteriously tenanted.

We sit within our cube of warmth and speed;
The road turns sharply to the right, and I
Sway to your side; the roughness of your coat
Brushes my face and I forget the need
Of balancing erect; the night slips by;
The journey's end is blissfully remote.

Knight Errant

Margot's face was small and merry;
Margot's laugh was quick and low;
And she knew all sorts of very
Curious things no girl should know.

Margot's house was most erratic,
With five casual purple towers,
And her garden bore exotic,
Careless and unusual flowers.

Ulric viewed the purple walls
And the sinuous, flower-hung tree,
Doubting to find within those halls
A simple hospitality.

But six fights that day had tired
Ulric slightly; it was late;
Man and horse were much bemired
And they felt the armor's weight.

There was food and drink in plenty;
Ulric stayed there all that night
And the next, and maybe twenty ...
Found his hostess most polite.

Once they lay in tangled fashion
On the grass and watched the moon;
Ulric had dined well; his passion
Felt the moment opportune.

Occasionally almost any
Woman's tact displays a flaw;
Margot made one joke too many,
And he thought of Ursula.

Ursula, who never troubled
To be witty or exact,
Whose constant conversation bubbled
Pointless, placid, matter-of-fact.

Women, if they will, can tell
When a lover's burning low.
Margot did a miracle,
Held her tongue and let him go.

Backward glancing once, he saw
Margot blurred through shallow tears,
Then rode home to Ursula
And scarcely thought of her for years.

Margot, who had never wept,
Groped blindly to the turret stair,
Up to her empty chamber crept
And found no laughter waiting there.

Three hundred moons have swelled and burst.
Old Ulric and his stout old wife
Walk heavily on their lawn. His first
Misdeed was eke his last, for life.

The moon shines wildly in his eyes
And lights a memory dim and faint.
He says, to Ursula's surprise,
"The old house needs a coat of paint.

"I never have liked that gray stone;
It seems so bleak; it lacks all cheer.
Let's paint the place a brighter tone.
Purple is nice, I think, my dear!"

A note that she has never heard
Thrills in his aging voice, and she
Wrinkles her lids, and says no word
But looks at him suspiciously ...

Eke: *(obsolete) also, in addition to.*

Moonin'

There's a boy an' a girl up there in the hay.
Shall I order 'em off or leave 'em lay?
    Gosh, but the moon is big tonight
    An' the air still warm - been a scorchin' day.

C'mon now, spose'n that was my gal
Layin' up there by the hoss corral -
    That moon ain't green cheese; it's plumb red -
Almost sorry it ain't little Sal.

Twisted up in her old wheel chair,
Never no straws in her pretty hair.
    Sly old Jeer on his round red face.
Mebbe it's wrong, but I can't care.

There's Right an' there's Wrong; I sucked that in
With my mother's milk; heerd a lot about Sin,
    Go on an' leer; I know how you feel!
An' I raised my fambly like I'd been.

But now there's times I ain't so all-fired
Sure as I was - shucks! I'm just tired
    Funny for moonlight to seem so hot
Bossin' that worthless galoot I've hired.

Them two young things still there in the hay
An' me here moonin'. Been a hard day.
    Comin', Sally; ain't the moon pretty tonight?
Oh, goldern it, leave 'em lay!

Almost a Memory

Once, in the velvet dark of early spring,
My path led through an orchard, and I went
'Neath massed invisible whiteness; the rich scent
Of lavish boughs in tender blossoming
Sank in my heart to half forgotten tears
And half remembered joy, in silence fraught
With echoes of a voice once loved, forgot,
Low-tuned beneath the stridence of the years.

Lightly a bough caressed me, murmuring this
On breath of sweetness: One has loved you well
In such a darkness. Silken petals fell
Across my cheek; the touch was like a kiss.
Draw near, lost love, wherever you may be.
By fragrance I may dream you back to me.

Stridence: *The quality of being loud, shrill, piercing or rough-sounding.*

Moon Driven

You came upon me like a gathering wave,
Too far, as yet to gauge its depth and power.
To gamble with the ocean for an hour
Demands high stakes; for once I will be brave.
I will await your onrush where I stand,
Moon-driven one, until you break complete,
To curl in gentle reverence at my feet
Or lay me spent, bedraggled, on the sand.

Sometime, mid the warm scent of yellow broom
On summery hillsides suddenly I shall burn
With deepcut memory of the sea, shall yearn
Douthily for the coldness and the spume;
And when the moon calls, I shall have to learn
To draw the shades and sit in a dim room.

Douthily: *Thirstily, with thirst.*

New Year's Eve of 1905

The New Year's Eve of nineteen hundred five
my boyfriend took me to attend his church
to spend the closing hour upon our knees.
Not that we were devout; it was a thing
to do if we could not afford a dance.

When we left the warm church we found the night
had turned to freezing, with a bitter breeze.
The streetcars had stopped running; we must walk.
Alone, he could have run to warm himself
but I could not. My teeth began to chatter,
I moaned complaint. He took his jacket off
and wrapped it round me. I suppose I thanked him
and I accepted it and went on moaning.
He, in his shirtsleeves, was anxious about me.
When we came to my door and said goodnight
he kissed me with especial tenderness
as if his generosity in some way
had made him love me more. The kiss was awkward
for both our sets of teeth were chattering,
but I've remembered it through all these years.

The years are many; each one has brought change.
We who were girl and boy in that old world
have watched the changes and we always try
to hope the next one will be for the better.
Perhaps the girls are hardier today
and boys less chivalrous; I do not know.
They do not speak our language, nor we theirs.
But still the years maintain the ancient round,
each new one bringing with it a new hope
to us who greet its coming with a prayer.

The Man in the Moon

Slow circling through the purple arc of night,
A Face, ghost pale, gleams sinister, serene,
A changeless halted miracle; its sheen
Floods down the slumberous hills in cool blue light.
Dead eyes, twin graves of vision, blankly stare
In answer to a questioning upthrust
Toward bafflement; that silent silver crust
Veils ashen caverns, sadly still and bare.

The livid mouth smiles tolerant, deadly wise,
As who has tasted deep and richly quaffed
And quaffing died and dying richly laughed
Transfixed in mockery of paradise.
Quick, love, the curtains close together fling;
Shield our live kiss from this insensate Thing!

***

Quaf: *to drink deeply and heartily.*

A Whimper

If you should kiss me would a ghost be laid?
I'd be afraid to have you love me now;
Not for the pain — indeed I wonder how
Pain could affect us — but I'd be afraid
That my lips meeting yours would be as cold
And dry as hoar on winter leaves; you see,
Don't you, how poor a sadness that would be,
A thinly tragic tale too often told.

And then again, a ghost may easily prove
A tender lissome thing, with all the grace
And charm of the solid living body missed
By its solidity. You mentioned love?
Yes, hasn't it led us both a merry chase?
No, I will not — well then, if you insist ...

Hoar: *Ice crystals from water vapor forming a white deposit on exposed surfaces when the air is cold and moist.*

Inconsistency

I was false to my soul today,
    Little, unworthy, untrue,
        And my soul stands up and accuses me,
        But I hardly dare its face to see,
    For its face is the face of you.

If you should come to me now,
    For all that wistful face,
        I should feint and parry and thrust, no doubt,
        As if my love were a fencing bout,
    Wherein truth had no place.

"It was all in self-defense,"
    I can hear my sore heart say;
        Yet your eyes were kind and your friendship pure,
        And your heart held no though of war, I'm sure,
    But I was false to my soul today.

To a Greek Head

Alive in stone, impenetrably cool,
    That stately face looks down from Grecian days
    As from a tower; with blank experienced gaze,
Too placid to be less than beautiful.
Athena, glowing from the sculptor's tool,
    Immortally through centuries, to raise
    In men a brief serenity, portrays
Her power where Athens never dreamed to rule.

To greater times and hero-loves belong
    Those full firm lips, wisely, maturely chaste,
    Marred to more beauty, scornful of complaint
And rapture; does that silent hidden tongue
    Beyond the unsmiled smile, securely taste
    A flavor of voluptuous restraint?

Two Loves

In the far pale sky was born a Love,
    A white and gracious thing;
For a moment poising itself above,
    Then bending its snowy wing,
        It drifted downward, silently,
            To the hill-top's welcoming.

It breathed content in that lofty air,
    Content with the hills and sky;
But it saw earth's valleys, and they were fair,
    So leaving the mountain high
        And drifting downward heavily
            Sank to earth with a cry.

For down in the valley the frail white thing
    Was trampled and choked and marred,
And the lowland mists were gathering,
    And life was hard -- so hard --
        It struggled a little, then wearily
            Lay very still on the sward.

Sward: *an area of ground covered with short grass.*

Down in the valley was born a Love,
    A humble and hardy thing,
Scarce knowing itself, till from above
    It once heard an angel sing,
        And reaching up half-timidly
            Found wild flowers blossoming.

Then Love knew itself, left the plains behind,
    And growing more brave and strong,
With a firm glad faith in all its kind
    It climbed the hills with a song,
        Going forward bravely, cheerily,
            Though the way was hard and long.

At last Love stood on the summit's height,
    Where the air was pure and rare,
And the plains below were a lovely sight,
    But heaven was more than fair;
        And the earth-born Love stood reverently
            For the wonder of life was there.

Unexpressed

The mirror pictures of my usual day
My heart holds up to you as in a glass;
A sudden flight of sunshine over grass,
A gift of roses, or mire of clay
I share with you; you walk along my way
Through all the moments, leaden, golden, brass;
And not an hour of all the hours that pass
But sees you sharing in all work and play.

And now I see your face, the voice falls dumb;
Your eyes strike silence to my fluent speech;
And we can only stand here and await
The parting that inevitably will come

Swathed in our mute rebellion, suffering each
Dull misery of the inarticulate.

Dark Water

Visions and voices from the spirit deeps,
Voices and visions beckon the senses in;
Wraiths of desire, pale, tenuous and thin,
The while the guardian of the castle sleeps,
Woo us in dreams, and wooing surely win;
Back from the dawn the pregnant darkness creeps;
And each man in his treasure casket keeps
Locked the white rose of Lady Might-have-been.

As twilight youth merges in sunlit age
Reflected broken in the pebbled stream,
Three faery lights, rose-veiled, uncertain, gleam,
An untrod path, a white unwritten page
And kisses like water in a thirsty dream,
Tasted, but never captured to assuage.

No Candle Burning

I keep no candle burning now
To lure a moth, or pay a vow,
Or beautify an evening meal,
Or melt red wax to drip a seal.

For seals are brittle things to break
And meals are only meat and cake
And moths will fan a flame and go,
And as for vows - oho!

Shopworn

Clear eyed I search the sources of desire.
The faded petals of a passion-flower
Droop, and a new bud opens in that hour,
And changing fuel feeds a permanent fire.
"If this be love I never loved before,"
You said, thinking to please me with that word,
But pity for forgotten loves you slurred
Is set between us like a bolted door.

Something withholds from me the power to trust,
Forget, and trust again as fresh hearts may,
An undercurrent in your tenderness
That bids me fear to love you as I must,
A wariness in your eyes, and dare I say
A schooled perfection in your least caress.

I Warn You

Sometime you'll stay away so long
That when you do come back
You will find hanging on my door
A grim rosette of black.

And will you lift your hand and knock
And ask to see the dead?
No, you will turn and walk away
With all the words unsaid.

A Song

Sweet, oh sweet, your eyes are gray
    With mockery in their light
And I am warned to go my way
Yet while their magic bids me stay
    I yield me to its might.

Sweet, my sweet, I once have dreamed
    They held life's joy for me
Once, when the moon above us beamed
A vague elusive softness seemed
    Within their depths to be.

Sweet, oh sweet, your eyes are gray
    And baffling in their light,
Yet if one love glance in them lay
I would their lightest look obey
    And deem the mandate right.

Oh now I lay my armor down,
    Your victory is complete;
I love your smile, I love your frown,
I kiss the border of your gown,
    My heart is at your feet,
    Sweet, my sweet.

Aftermath

You might be in any one of the cars that pass;
I could glimpse your face in the window of a train;
I could stroll through a park, see you stretched on the grass,
Then walk straight on and never see you again.

You were just at the other end of a telephone line,
I could dial a number and your voice would be there;
For years I have wondered how it would answer mine;
For all those years it was something I did not dare.

Exit Line

When at the last my heart shall be wrung dry
Of every tremulous tear, I have it planned
To look you gently, calmly in the eye
And say to you, "My, dear, I understand."
Spare us all further words; just let me go
Quietly and in order, with a shred
Of dignity to wrap around me; so
I shall be decent, though uncomforted.

Now gravely I can bid farewell to fear
And happiness and pain. I shall be free
Of torment and of hope, and you, my dear.
All this with poise unbroken and polite,
Securely held till I am out of sight.

Chess or Contract

Confess, you start a game with every stranger
Which seldom goes beyond the opening play;
A glance refuses, interest falls away
From subtle invitation or from danger
He lacks in skill, or will, or situation;
You close the board and lay away the men
— Until it's time to set them out again —
With mild and long-accustomed resignation.
Thrice, perhaps, in this lifetime, some one answers
With all the proper moves — if you are wise
You crash the pieces to the floor, and rise
And flee as from dire peril. Ah, romancers,
Why dare misfortune's cruelest of crosses?
Forbear, and be content with little losses?

Incomplete

You do not know the worst life has to offer
If you have never lingered in the rain
And cold, outside a glowing window-pane,
To watch the firelight beckon on the floor,
Knowing that your own hand has barred the door;
You do not know how much your heart can suffer.

4

PEOPLE

Herself

All day, and every day for thirty years
she lay on her back and waited.

    She could hold
a forked stick in her hand, with which to turn
the pages of a book propped up before her
and read through thick-lensed glasses; or she talked
cheerily with her friends.

    Then there were meals;
they were events in her life; and she was proud
that she could feed herself. But when she drank
one had to hold the cup; her small gnarled hand
would not quite bend around it.

    People said,
those who had known her thirty years ago,
that as a girl she played the violin
promisingly. She never mentioned music,
though she would talk of every other thing.

She spoke with confidence of getting well
"Some day," she said, "I shall stand up and walk.
I'll walk straight to the window and look out.
Oh, I'll surprise you all!"

    She did surprise us.
One morning we looked in and she was gone,
and very little trace was left of all
that could be called herself. Did she, we wondered,
stand up, and stretch, and walk across the room,
and look out at the sunrise, and go on?

Her Picture

They took her picture on her wedding day.
He had it framed and proudly points it out
To visitors; perhaps he does not see
Anything in that picture but her beauty.
And she was beautiful, more so, they say,
Than any colorless photograph could show.
I never saw her . . . You see, she died
When I was born. The way I understand it,
I was his flesh too, and the two of us
Were more than she could tolerate and live.
Do you suppose she has forgiven me?
Not him, of course, and not herself, but I
Committed no intentional harm. I wish
Only that she may go free and be at peace.

Empty Chairs

The wicker chairs creak
and rustle as I pass them
in the darkened room.

I would like to say
to whatever may sit there:
Please don't be disturbed!

I dare not say it.
I am afraid of speaking
to an empty chair.

A Simple Man

He used to say, "Well I should kiss a pig."
and laugh as though he's made a brand-new joke;
a kindly, simple man, generous and big
and fond of home and kindly simple folk.

One night as he was taking his necktie off,
"Where have you been?" his wife sleepily said
between a yawn and an absent little cough.
He looked at her and did not come to bed.

He put his necktie on and left the place,
left his two children, left his church and friends.
Months afterward it seems he had the grace
to send his wife a word. No one defends
him; people used to wonder, but his face
is now forgotten so the story ends.

Martyr Complex

He had a martyr complex. That's to say
He had but scant capacity for the lies
Men feed themselves; each niggling compromise
With self-respect forced him nearer to the day
Of ultimate choice, whether he should obey
The pull of his own conscience, or be wise
In petty things. So it was no surprise
To find himself against the world, at bay.

Chill anguish of a desperate loneliness
Beset him. Then he suddenly ceased to dread
The flavor of the vinegar and myrrh,
And peace the smug half-hearted never guess
Upheld him as he set his feet to treat
The path of Galileo and Pasteur.

Is That So

She has many friends, old and new
who enjoyed talking with her
and felt that they knew her well
If you told her that you made butter
when you lived on a farm in your youth
She would say, "Is that so!"
in a tone which implied
that this was the one thing needed
to complete her education
A large part of her popularity
rests on those three words.

To A.J.C.

He is, in devious Californian way,
Frank as the sky and subtle as the earth,
Apt to be rocked by Rabelaisian mirth
Warmed to the core by golden rainless days . . .
He reads thus far, increasing in amaze,
And I can hear his merry chuckled curse,
"Well, I'm damn glad that sonnet is no worse!"
(I'd vowed to write a sonnet in his praise.)

His casual kisses fan a little glow
Of friendliness; not every man would be
So casual; nor do I fail to comprehend
His dash of boyish braggadocio;
Life, you old bungler, treat him tenderly;
Keep him a boy until the very end.

Rabelaisian: *1) marked by gross robust humor, extravagance of caricature, or bold naturalism; 2) of, relating to, or characteristic of Rabelais or his works. Francois Rabelais (b 1483-1490, d 1553) was a French Renaissance writer, physician, monk and Greek scholar, most famous for his stories of two giants - a father, Gargantua, and his son, Pantagruel. Written in an amusing and satirical style and containing crudity, off-color humor, vulgar insults and violence, they were banned by academics at the Sorbonne University in Paris and by the Roman Catholic Church.*
Braggadocio: *the annoying or exaggerated talk of someone who is trying to sound very proud or brave; empty boasting.*

The Office Secretary

All day she deals with people;
prosperous and aggressive;
poor and intimidated;
or run-of-the-mill decent
with small emergencies.
She deals with them, not always sure
of being right, but sustained
by the stiff costume of authority.
When the day's work is over
she looks into the mirror,
a shy, modest girl,
viewing the face life has put on her,
comely enough, but is it her own?

To Art Eisler

The soul whose earthly time is spent in music,
on entering the hereafter, finds itself
ready, attuned to heavenly harmony;
prepared to join creation's orchestra;
joyously welcomed in by fellow craftsmen
and comfortably at home among all splendors.

Art Eisler: Accomplished musician and composer who lived in Marin County, California, probably at least from the 1940's until his death in 1974. He was a contemporary and friend of Sibyl's.

To M.D.

Tempered and seasoned as your violin
Taut as the fine slip shaft that is its bow,
Polished as its clear surface, do you know
The unplayed melodies that lie within?
O slender Anglo-Saxon blond, I hear
Wild music underneath your smooth, cool tones;
The Druids march; the Celtic banshee moans;
The harp of Wales chants prophecy severe.

A sense of fate broods over you. No knight
Can wear such shining armor on his breast
And yet escape attack from life's crude lance.
Be troubadour, and in your music's light
Brave voice will be your weapon and your best
Defense against all challenge and mischance.

The Poet

He tasted peace only when he had wrought
To sculptured rhythm the life that in him stirred,
And carved in crystal for the fluid thought
The accurate, inevitable word.

To Sara Teasdale

You spread a soul on paper, line by line,
And in your poignant smiling verse a horde
Of inarticulate women find the word
For a stifled heart's release and anodyne.
An aqueduct of universal wine,
Channel of life's transfusions, you have poured
Your full libation to a greedy lord
That I may drain the last red drop of mine.

Lady of vinted lovers, do not fear
Reproachful eyes of ghosts appraising you;
You will have learned through loving oft and long
That half forgotten loves can still be dear
And fused into yourself, most fixedly true
Those honored hearts distilled into a song.

Vint: *produce wine or an alcoholic beverage*
Anodyne: *a painkiller or medicine that relieves pain.*
Sara Teasdale (1884-1933): *An American lyric poet. She won the Pulitzer Prize in 1918 for her poetry collection "Love Songs".*

Marc

My grandson is a troubadour,
born to a foreign century.
He is encumbered with a store
of ancient skills and curious lore
not understood by me.

He strolls in, bearing on his back
the total of his worldly goods;
two instruments, a blanket pack,
bible and clothing in a sack
and a song to trade for food.

I know he has not long to stay;
a pressure and an urgent need
from long ago and far away
define his path. I can but say
a gracious, brief Godspeed.

Privacy Achieved

A buxom woman
With well groomed hair
And a proud walk;
When she sat at our table
She told us how much salt to eat
And how to chew our meat.
She went into the kitchen
And told the chef how to cook;
She went to the piano
And told the player:
Your ought to practice more.
At the bridge table
She gave lavish instruction.

Now, less buxom,
Hair hanging straight,
Shoulders less erect,
She eats alone at a small table,
An open book beside her plate.

Home-Coming

There's a warm pressure in the gusts
like blown velvet, ominously warm;
a few pale leaves take their last ride;
dust rises like a whorl of moonlight;
a tumbleweed is going somewhere
in a great hurry
and the clouds are busy.

Behind three squares of light
is peace
and a sweet wood fire.
Fasten the old doors securely;
they must not remember being trees.
And we will talk with the fire
until rain washes down the dark
and lays us quiet.

Rude Words

I was baptized with good words
and all my life they have poured over me
till I have become so saturated
that, on occasion, they even pour out of me.
Sometimes I feel like telling the preacher:
for God's sake say something new,
or shut up and let me think.

Grandma Eschews Parsley

Don't bother me with parsley, I find it hard to chew;
The flavor is peculiar, you'll admit;
They say it contains vitamins, and though this may be true
I'm not inclined to eat a pound of it.

There is a certain restaurant in one Bay Area city
Where they serve it made of plastic, I am told,
To decorate the salad, and though it may look pretty
It's not for the digestion of the old.

So feed it to the robot, who will munch it without thought
His dry synthetic hunger to abate.
There are mountains to be climbed and battles to be fought;
Don't bother to put parsley on my plate.

New England Ancestry

The tropic fish has color gay
And shape incredible;
The temperate fish is sober, gray,
Well-formed and edible.

And though my heart for strange warm seas
Vagrantly wishes,
Its fate must be the fate of these
Edible fishes!

Eschew: *To deliberately avoid using; abstain from.*

My Education
(Hieronymus Bosch)

"Hieronymus Bosch," the erudite visitor began,
his glance sweeping the circle of listeners.
I had seen the name in print, though uncertain
whether of theologian or trapeze performer,
so I lighted up my face and leaned forward
in an attitude of eager attention.
The great man favored me with the smile
that recognizes an intellectual compatriot
and addressed his ensuing remarks to me.
Thus I learned all I ever expect to know
of Hieronymus Bosch, whose name I now mention
with the easy familiarity of long acquaintance.
In this manner I obtained my education.

Hieronymus Bosch (1450 - 1516): *Dutch painter known for fantastic illustration of religious concepts and macabre depictions of hell.*

Place Names of Marin

The gentle, rhythmic place-names of Marin
Salute with music the accustomed ear;
There's Sausalito, like a mandolin,
And deep-toned Tiburon and Belvedere.

Attuned to melody like an ancient bell,
Ignacio and Novato seem to chime
With San Geronimo and San Rafael
The legend of an earlier, saintlier time.

Crisp overtones of Fairfax, Kentfield, Ross,
Larkspur, Mill Valley, breathe harmonic spice
Into unpatterned airs that play across
The somber dissonance of Tamalpais.

So let our children, wheresoe'er they be
On stranger shores, forever bear within
The homing heart's nostalgic memory
The gentle, rhythmic place-names of Marin.

Marin: *Marin County, California, just north of San Francisco. Sibyl lived in the city of Mill Valley in Marin County for much of her adult life.*

Mill Valley to Malibu

The gorgeous houses slide into
The sea that washes Malibu.

I live in a secluded alley
In a suburban town, Mill Valley.

I do not own a swimming pool;
My children go to public school.

I can't afford to travel jet
And haven't paid my taxes yet,
But I don't envy people who
Have stately homes in Malibu.

Malibu: *A small town on the Pacific Coast in Los Angeles County. Many expensive homes are built on the hillside overlooking the ocean. In 1978, heavy winter rains caused massive mudslides; many homes were damaged, some actually sliding down the hillsides.*

Why Bother

Why should I undergo the rigor
of improving my figure?
Of course, if I want to, I can
and maybe I would, for a man.
But with only a yellow cat
who doesn't give a meow whether I'm slim or fat,
who thinks me an angel of goodness
when I mix up his food mess,
and who considers me beautiful
when I keep his plate, as is my duty, full -
Well, there's more than one way of making life sweet.
Me — I eat!

Merry Christmas Happy New Year

I disapprove of Christmas cards
They come in stacks and bales
They clutter up the window sills
And overload the mails

But somehow at this time of year
One reaches out to friends
And though we send no Christmas card
Our friendship never ends

5

REGRET, PAIN & SORROW

Unfinished Story

His mouth was cold and weak against my breast,
the child I nursed an hour before he died,
still he drew milk; it was as though he tried
to take with him a little of the best
that this brief life had known, a tiny test
of tiny strength. He was to be denied
all greater challenge, to be set aside
and so inopportunely dispossessed.

Sometime, somewhere a great man will appear,
gladly conceived and nurtured by another.
Perhaps he tried to come to earth through me,
a shining light to sweep the darkness clear,
and I who might have been that happy mother
stand blindfold at the brink of mystery.

Hokku of Expectancy

The faint but potent
Atmospheric disturbance
Of a throbbing pulse

Seemed almost enough
To have precipitated
The desired presence;

For I could feel you,
Nebulous but imminent,
In every moment.

Hokku of Happiness

Come into this world
Born into a family,
But seek your kindred!

And having found them
Let your heart, hands, brain and time
Be at their service.

There's no other way
To circumvent nostalgia
And make happiness.

Hokku: *Same as haiku; a form of poetry with seventeen syllables, in three lines of five, seven, and five.*

Hokku for Tears

I see afar off
Pain, so beautiful, distant.
Ah, come not nearer!

This poor futile tear
Dries on the lash unuttered
To waste salt water.

Body, we are friends.
I give you fidelity
Until you fail me.

Patience, dignity,
A calm, self-contained spirit,
These are splendid words!

Huddle together,
Forlorn me, forlorn women,
And be still forlorn.

Hokku of Pain

There is in my heart
A morsel of hard substance
That resembles pain.

Throughout many years
This thing has been part of me
And all my living.

If you cut that heart
Open when I have left it
You may find a pearl.

Dawn Stirrings

A tremor pulses faintly on the clear
Dark air; the scented vine leaves sigh and shake;
The newborn roses tremble in its wake
And keep the silence of a holy fear;
And ears long aching of the stillness hear
A nameless stir; the night begins to break,
And eyes long weary of the darkness take
Heart in their vigil, that its end is near.

Roused to the whisper of a dawn half sped,
Small downy birdlings flutter in their nests;
There is no fluttering where my birdling rests
Dreamless within a covered satin bed,
But how the hollow place between my breasts
Throbs for the rounding of a little head.

Birdling: *a little bird; a nestling*

Has All Been Said

Has all been said that may be said, I wonder,
About the drift of birds across a sky
That floats in pools of golden clearness under
The arch of space? Now resolutely I
Crush this bright life of the spirit into words!
Wingless, I launch a song; a melody
Wavers, and that dark silent flow of birds
Reproves me for a brave futility.

Yet there is that for which I must be brave;
And if a flight of sunset birds, or a dune
That lifts its beach-flowered roundness in a suave
Silhouette, or a curled strand of virgin moon
Smile briefly on my harassed heart, I gain
One breath of peace, drawn clean across my pain.

A Happy Thought

Why should I allow pain to eat me
when, by fixing my attention
on the light-years to Betelgeuse,
I can become aware
how small is my sorrow?

How this would sustain me
if I could but forget
how infinitely smaller than my sorrow
am I!

Airless Night

An airless night
heavy with warm rain
and darkness thick with rude, uneasy spirits
crowding and jostling at the doors of flesh.

I lie awake and think of debts
and am afraid to dream.

Betelgeuse: *a large red supergiant star in the constellation Orion. It is the 9th brightest star in the night sky, about 640 light-years from Earth.*

Dream

My world had crashed in a mire
 of dust and tears.
I was not weeping, I was being
 wept,
shaken and shattered by a storm
 of grief
then — in two strong and gentle
 arms this small
lost creature was enfolded and
 sustained.
I clung, still weeping, but
 without despair,
I clung to that quiet strength
 and found myself
Sustained, enfolded, quieted,
 beloved.

The Bell Team

High in the air, on the swaying jolting seat
Of the big farm wagon, Susie loved to ride.
Her father smoked his corncob at her side.
Lurching around a bend, her little feet
And slip legs dangled wildly. Spicy heat
Rose up in waves from a horse's sweaty hide.
"The bay mare's conscientious, has some pride;
Get up, Joe! Pull your share, you lazy cheat."

The rhythmic jangle of the leader's bells
Flung out a warning for the road to hear it,
"Room for four horses and a load, my friend."
Now Susie, in the city where she dwells
Hears sometimes through its hollowness of spirit
Father's old bell team coming round the bend.

6

POLITICAL COMMENTARY

1940

Mother,
    what shall I do
When they put a gun in my hand?
Mother, I'm asking you;
Help me to understand.

My country,
    tell me true
If I pour out my blood
What will it do for you?
Will it make you strong and good?

Sweetheart,
    if I am killed
Because I am whole and sound
Will a weakling father your child
When I am underground?

God,
    when they took your son
And nailed him to a tree
Why didn't you give him a gun
Like the one they're handing me?

Berry Hill

The news reeked of death and carnage.
To get away from it all
a few of us left the city
for a week-end in a Sierra village.
Main Street had some tottering store-fronts
with a fading memory of commerce and gold dust,
and the brick walls of the Bank
which now enclosed a sizable pine tree.
The short street ended
at a sharp rise of ground.
"We call that Berry Hill,"
said the old-timer.

It was early for strawberries
but as I ascended the overgrown trail
I watched for low white blossoms.
Over the crest, dark trees gathered gloom;
two flat gray stones leaned toward me
with names and dates.
Beyond, a scattering of smaller stones
and unmarked concavities of ground
where my foot would not care to tread.

I retraced my steps
down the weedy trail,
past the Bank,
past the store-fronts;
and, for some obscure reason,
I did not tell my week-end friends
what fruit I had found
on Bury Hill.

Good News on the Radio

One child slain on the highway calls for pity;
One son destroyed in battle wrings the heart;
And yet they say, Rejoice! when a whole city
With men and sons and homes, is blown apart.
The enemy! they shout. And who is he?
The stranger, the barbarian, he whose way
Is not as Our Way, that's the enemy!
And I believe they lie, and lie for pay.

So I will spare my ears and turn the dial;
If I must suffer let it not be soon,
From hate-polluted air, for this short while
Let me escape their mouthings with a tune —
Spike Jones, for preference, whose ungodly noise
Makes mockery of all sorrows and all joys.

__Spike Jones__ (1911 - 1965) American musician and bandleader (Spike Jones and His City Slickers) specializing in satirical arrangements of popular songs and classical music. Ballads receiving the Jones treatment were punctuated with gunshots, whistles, cowbells and outlandish and comedic vocals.

Schweitzer

Has the Lord returned to earth
again in a manner unexpected?
Not in the air with a shout
and fanfare of heavenly trumpet
but in the guise of a modest man,
bearing a rich heritage,
who looked at a lost world
still ready to crucify him,
and then sought out the lowliest
of the suffering poor
and quietly gave them his life.

This time he needs no Twelve
to spread the word of his coming.
In every tongue the articulate world
speaks his name with reverence
if not with understanding.

Will there come a time
when, in the midst of frantic pain,
the sudden message will shine out:
He is here!

Albert *Schweitzer (1875 - 1965), French-German theologian, organist, writer, humanitarian, philosopher and physician. He was awarded the Nobel Peace Prize in 1952 for his philosophy "Reverence for Life" expressed in many ways, but most famously in founding (1914) and sustaining (until the mid-50's) the Albert Schweitzer Hospital in Lambarene (now Gabon). After WWII, from 1952 until his death, he worked to eradicate nuclear tests and nuclear weapons.*

Resistance

To recapitulate the sorry tale
of all the ills attending civilization
seems not worth while — which causes me to fail
of taking part in many a conversation.

I will not send my mind down that dark trail
of anger, hopelessness and degradation,
while there are airs to breathe and seas to sail,
people to love and moments of creation.

New Orleans, 1960

I sent my little girl to school today,
My little girl — and her first day at school.
I scrubbed her small dark face until it shone
And tied white ribbons in her curly hair
And sent her off, escorted by police.

She turned to smile and wave her hand to me,
So small, so gentle, and so unafraid.
One must have faith in law, and faith in God;
That is what I have taught my little girl.
I wonder now--should I have·taught her fear?

New Orleans School Crisis: Under court-ordered desegregation, on November 14, 1960, Ruby Bridges was escorted by armed federal marshals into her new school in New Orleans. Pictures published world-wide showed her walking up the steps with white ribbons in her hair.

Unfit

"Give me the children!" cried the angry father
Before the judge. "She is not fit, I tell you,
To care for them and teach them. She is — look —
I found these on her desk!" And he held out
Two books for the inspection of the court.
The judge glanced down and nodded, for he knew
The books by title — not that he had ever
Sullied his sight with their abhorrent contents —
One was by Lenin, one by Marx. The man
Continued, "She does not believe in God!
Ask her, your honor!" And the judge was shocked.

The woman spoke: "Your honor, do not take
My little children from me! Look, are they
Neglected, underfed, ill-clothed, untaught?
And is there any other in this world
Tho will love and nurture them as well as I?"

"Are you a communist?" the judge inquired
Sternly, "Would you teach these two to be
Communists?" The horror of that word
Lost nothing on his tongue.

            She hesitated.
"Sir, I am not a member of the party.
Being only one of those who seek, and read,
And study every scheme that promises
To help the world and somehow make for justice.
And I would teach my children to do this,
And try to keep their minds unspoiled by fear,
Alert to love the truth. Can this be wrong?"

He shook his head. The woman was too glib.
Besides, she spoke of justice — that's a matter
Which should be left to experts. He passed on
To surer ground. "Do you believe in God?
"Say yes or no!" She was silent for a moment.
How could she, even for her children's sake
Profess her faith in a God who would allow
Himself to be dragged about in such a way?
If she could only tell them, could explain
That she believed in justice, truth, and love,
Which Christians claim essential to their God,
Perhaps she could make them see — but time was passing —
She had but one poor word allowed. She drew
Upon her soul for courage, and said, "No."

The judge then solemnly, and with some pity —
For even communists and atheists
May have some measure of natural affection,
And the woman's stubborn face was very white —
Pronounced his verdict: "I find you unfit
To undertake the care of these young minds
The children are awarded to their father."
And added, as if sentencing to death,
"And may the Lord have mercy on your soul!"

"Unfit" is based on an incident in "The March of Time", a weekly radio documentary and dramatization news series (1931-1945) and monthly short film series shown in movie theaters from 1935 - 1951. Both sponsored by Time Inc. It exposed and attacked fascism and communism.

He Stirreth Up the People

Comrade Jesus, carpenter,
Humbly walked the dusty street,
Spoke good tidings to the poor,
Gave them fish and bread to eat,
Touched their wounds with healing hand,
Listened fairly when they spoke,
Seldom found a trusty friend
Save among the working folk.
Mighty men with hides to save,
Rich, respectable, and fat,
Saw the poor grow strong and brave,
Crucified him -- just for that.

From Luke 23:5: "And they were more fierce, saying, He stirreth up the people, teaching throughout all Jewry, beginning from Galilee to this place." (King James Bible).

Whither From Earth

A friendly planet, where
such as we can find footing,
they say is rather rare.
With all our plundering, looting
and stupid hate run wild
what child
will dare to hazard birth
on what we make of Earth?

Shall we be, then,
stray points of consciousness
that once were man and woman,
afloat in spatial wilderness,
seeking for hospitable soil
where once again
we can begin the long slow toil
toward being human?

The Piano

For years I have stood, and still I stand,
    Patient and worn and dumb,
Awaiting the touch of a master's hand,
    Why does it never come?
        There's a soul that lurks in these hidden strings,
        Who will give voice to its murmurings?

White hands have fluttered in fitful songs
    Over my ivory keys;
For a poor dumb soul that yearns and longs
    What sign of hope have these?
        I offered a treasure to them, and they
        Flouted the gift and went their way.

The years have flown as this year is flying
    And I am growing old;
From the unused fire in my heart strings is dying
    My soul is growing cold,
        Yet it could be warmed by the touch I await;
        Oh, master, come e're it be too late.

Hark, he is coming -- I feel his tread.
    It thrills through the waiting strings;
And the fainting soul that almost fled
    Wakes into life and sings;
        For the weary waiting now is past,
        And I feel the master's hand at last.

He came -- he played, and not for long
    Was the vibrant ecstasy,
But I am content to have sung my song
    And to own one memory.
        Let these useless strings this moment sever,
        The soul that has spoken lives forever.

Fate and Love

I am resigned to be with the people who read
And write
And think
And know themselves.
For they are my people,
And away from them I am alien.
I did not make it so.
I ask not to go high among them,
I would rather stay where I can reach my hand
Over the border
To grasp the hand
Of some dear alien who reaches toward us.
I would hold his hand tightly,
That perhaps through me
Some of his love and humanness
May reach my people.
I would look into his eyes
With a long look
That perhaps I may give him
Some of the inspiration of my people.
Sorrow may come from it --
For when was love or inspiration without that?
But if through my sorrow
Or his sorrow
Come some good to my people
Or his people,
Then nothing is hopeless,
For the highest joy is in sacrifice.

From California

When swallows fail to come to Capistrano
and the butterflies are lost to Monterey
and redwoods lie in ashes in Butano
and herring boycott San Francisco Bay
when deer no longer nibble at our roses
and curious little faces of raccoons
no longer haunt our windows as day closes
and sand verbenas vanish from the dunes;
then let each lonely soul turn to its lover
and whisper Come with me a journey far,
as hand in hand we set forth to discover
a dwelling place on some unravaged star.

Swallows at Capistrano: *Starting early in the 20th century, migrating cliff swallows arrived on March 19th every year and nested at Mission San Juan Capistrano (San Juan Capistrano, California).*
Butterflies in Monterey: *Every winter, from October to February, thousands of butterflies make a stop in Monterey during their migration to warmer climates.*
Redwoods in Butano: *Butano Park, California west of San Jose. Butano State Park, created in 1957, boasts a redwood forest, as do nearby Portola Redwoods and Big Basin Redwoods State Parks.*
Herring in San Francisco Bay: *Each year from December to March, the Pacific herring (a fish similar to a sardine) swarms into San Francisco Bay by the millions.*

7

PHILOSOPHICAL REFLECTIONS

Too Late Smart

Throughout a life of jolts and bumps
I might have spared myself some lumps
if I had earlier learned to say,
"You may be right; let's try your way."

Tell the World

After long arduous study
and a course of elevated thinking
you arrive at an important truth
and you may stand
at a crowded street corner
shouting this important truth to the world
only to discover
that every passerby
has known it for a long time.

The Philosopher

Naked he stood, and missed his morning plunge
Pondering the sea-born marvel of a sponge.

A Square Inch of Space

It was satisfying
to slay a red deer with our own hands,
soften the hide with our strong teeth,
sharpen a small bone on a bit of flint,
punch holes for a shapely seam
and lace it flat, patting the stitches
into a smooth braid.

In the time of the Crusades
we eased our forsaken hearts
with intricate designs in bright wool
and hemmed the sturdy linens
that decked our lonely beds.

Within a square inch of space
a woman may travel widely,
leaving imperishable tracks.
In that small, quiet world
is no sound but the purr
of thread slipping through cloth
and the castanet of the thimble.
Angels may dance gravely
on the point of a needle
to the music of slow thoughts.

From hand to hand, along the centuries,
reaches the thread, unbroken.

The Crusade Spirit

In the flow of circumstances
the cause once holy
fades away,
failing or succeeding.
Reality, survival,
is in the crusade spirit.

Terrible Words

He saw, as in a dream,
humanity gathered
before the great throne,
each soul receiving to itself
a judgment, a penalty.
To him came the terrible words
that smote him to the dust:
You are one of the wisest; be a leader.

Pastime

When even tragedy fades out
And joy is far behind
To marvel what it's all about
May occupy the mind.

Pastime: *An activity that someone does regularly for enjoyment rather than work; a hobby*

Truth

If you would know truth
ask of an eminent man
who is very wise.
He can use a thousand words
to say: I don't know.

A Small Song

The string I touch is a gentle string,
A few pizzicato notes
That will not be heard when the woodwinds sing,
The cymbals clash and the brasses fling
A blare from their great brave throats.

But I know my notes and am glad to be
In the place where I belong.
For the ordered sweep of the symphony
Is perfectly ordered because of me
And my small pizzicato song.

Pizzicato: *(music) a note that is played on a stringed instrument by plucking instead of using a bow.*

Fugue by Wilhelm Friedmann Bach

You, down the centuries,
hear me!

I am the son of my father,
but also myself, a man, and
(God help me, piping against such thunder)
a musician.

You will be singing new songs
after your new fashion.
You may say: Oh, a fugue!
But I pray you listen
and hear, through the pattern
that he has stamped on me,
my own voice,
my own song!

Wilhelm Friedmann Bach (1710 - 1784): *Composer and son of the (more famous composer) Johann Sebastian Bach.*

An Article of Furniture

An old piano comes to have
a sort of soul — at least
it can hardly fail to gather
some accretion of humanity
for good or ill. Consider the tears
that have seeped through its key-board
to be embalmed in dust;
the violences of fist and elbow
its ivories have endured.

It might even, having lost hope,
acquire a sense of humor.
One family used to raise the lid
to let a kitten pounce
on the bouncing hammers.
That piano bore scars
where infant legs had kicked their way
gradually down to the pedals.

Another once stood as a barrier
between two terrified people
who dared not touch each other.
It never stayed in tune afterward.

A tiny piano stands
in the back of the store—
one hundred and twenty five years old, they say.
Daylight shows through the back
and most of the hammers play
two tones at once (believe me
if all those endearing young charms).
It will be bought for rosewood
and gutted to make a writing desk.

Oh, my gleaming new grand,
be humble.

"those endearing young charms" *references a song written in 1808 by Irish poet Thomas Moore, the theme of which is that love endures regardless of how the loved person looks. It is thought that Moore wrote the poem for his wife, who was badly scarred by smallpox.*

My Pearls

How I loved them -- my pearls -- shining rose and white,
    With kind little beamings,
    And strange little gleamings,
And a sweet serene light.

I had toiled for each gem such a weary while!
    I had worked, I had yearned,
    I had loved; I had earned
The reward of their smile.

There were all in the world that could make me glad,
    And comfort they brought,
    For each pearl was a thought --
They were all that I had.

Give them forth to the world? That could I not do.
    Even friends could not feel
    All the truth they reveal,
(For their luster seemed true.)

I looked at my pearls shining rose and white
    And they glowed faint as dreamings
    And vague little seemings --
They were losing their light!

Then in anguish I took them and cast them forth
    For swine to tramp over
    And foul earth to cover
'Twas all they were worth.

Then my dull eyes were touched—and I knew my brothers!
    And I learned that a treasure
    Only brings us full measure
As we trust it to others.

(An Answer)

The wounded soldier, dying for a creed,
    Has grasped a part of the Eternal Truth;
And thou in thy wise reasoning indeed
    Hast touched the side most obvious to youth.

The rage and sin of battle smite thy heart,
    It seems a cruel wrong that blood must flow.
Both war and peace bear their appointed part,
    In that great Purpose which no man may know.

The peace thou cravest has its given share
    And all things sweet and pleasant do their part,
But can we, all unknowing, stand and dare
    To judge the motives of the Maker's heart?

Shall we set up our standard as His guide
    And say to Him --- "Because we cannot know
How war and suffering are justified,
    We hold ourselves more righteous than Thou,"

Even with our narrow view of human life
    We see that sorrow has a natural place;
No great growth comes without some pain and strife,
    And suffering is all the blessing of our race.

The dying soldier lying on the field
    Is wiser in his simple faith than Thou;
He feels the great Eternal Love and yields,
    Content to leave some things unanswered now.

E'en through the battle's blood and smoke and din,
    He feels the hidden motive of his Lord,
And -- Love ordaining -- even seeming sin
    May fill its purpose to fulfill His word.

Kings 1:1-4

Abishag the Shunammite,
with body warm and white,
lay beside the king;
and David, who was old,
impotent and cold,
lay shivering.

Under the heavy coverlet
of wool and silk,
from her young flesh the sweat
started, warm as milk.

Mindful of her duty,
not to be wasted,
she curled close to his side,
but her beauty
went untasted.
Why do they bother me
with a woman! in his heart he cried
petulantly.

And when he saw that she slept
he sighed, then smiled,
and carefully crept
to the far side of the bed,
not to disturb the child;
and there he kept
vigil, uncomforted.

So Abishag the Shunammite
while all of one night
was spent,
slept with the king,
the poor old king,
impotent,
shivering.

Forbidden Fruit

Under glass,
On a shelf,
Fruit, immortally rose and gold,
Looms large through alcohol,
Forever untasted.
The garden spills other fruit,
Slightly speckled,
Slightly wormy perhaps,
But sweet enough.
Let us keep the one perfect thing
Under glass,
On a shelf.

Wholesome Fun

Work, in itself, is a pleasant thing
but when it comes to playing
I'm sorry, but I cannot care
for football or crocheting.

Dolls and bridge parties leave me cold;
for golf I've no desire.
The only toy worth playing with
is fire.

Babel

Mesopotamia, the level plain
between the rivers, as its name implies,
saw an ambitious race of men arise,
ingenious and resourceful sons of Cain
who in their pride and skill of hand were fain
with brick and mortar and bold enterprise
to build a tower and pierce the very skies
and challenge all the gods of that domain.

The gods, when first they noticed, were amused
then irritated by the impertinence
of a threatening ant-hill. Striking to the heart
of man's conspiracy, they first confused
then broke his power of speech, destroyed its sense
and mankind, chattering madly, fell apart.

A Sower

A sower did go forth to sow;
and what he sowed he did not know
for from his hand he dropped no seeds
but scattered song and smiles and deeds
which from his natural soul did flow.
He reckoned not of birds or weeds
or stony ground, or rake and hoe;
he was contented forth to go
and sow.

8

PLANTS, ANIMALS & NATURE

The Ginkgo Tree

The young leaves on a ginkgo tree
Are not quite as young leaves should be.
They are such frail and new-born things;
Each moist green frond so curls and clings;
Fern-changelings taken unaware,
Forlorn and wistful maidenhair.

Oh, I know ferns and I know trees,
But I am strange to such as these.
And so, upon this wild spring day,
There's fear abroad, and I must say
That young leaves on a ginkgo tree
Are not quite what young leaves should be.

Survival

The lineage of the ginkgo tree
Reaches beyond antiquity.

Its ferny foliage bent before
The clumsy prowling dinosaur.

Earth viewed his passing without grief
But cherishes the ginkgo leaf.

Ginkgo biloba: *Also known as maidenhair tree. Endangered species. Considered to be the earth's oldest tree.*

In a Garden

Sunshine like a warm hand fell on my shoulder;
brown soil smitten with water exhaled a song;
linnets in tall geraniums chattered infinitely;
flowering pomegranates decked themselves in fruitless scarlet;
red ants were faithful to pastoral duties about the roses;
a thirsty and furtive toad bided the heat with patience.
Thus the garden spoke civilly
and this dumb creature within it
heard, and made no answer.

Fern Fingers

The fern holds up fragile hands,
delicate and lavish,
with a casual number
of blind green fingers;
for warmth, coolness,
moisture, leaf-mold,
offering its price
of verdure.
Poor, brief bargaining against the day
when fingertips shall be
brown, shriveled, impotent
to give or to implore.

Verdure: *lush, green vegetation.*
Linnet: *a small brown and gray finch with a reddish breast and forehead.*
Bided (bide): *to bear, endure or tolerate.*

Antaeus

Yesterday I was lying in a wood;
the yellow sunlight filtered through the trees
and laid its dappled pattern on my knees
in areas of warm and cool; the good
firm earth pressed comfortably to my feet
who had been homesick; so I lay complete
and listened to the earth, and was renewed.

Green Things

Mint and cress and mimulus
With alders overhead,
These are things to fly to
When the day goes dead.

Little things to hoard away
In safe and secret places,
To savor when one wearies
Of wheels and talk and faces.

Cress: A plant of the cabbage family, typically having small white flowers and pungent leaves. Some kinds are edible and are eaten raw as salad.
Mimulus: Also called Monkey Flower. A native North American wildflower. Blossoms are often spotted and multicolored and tend to look like a monkey's face.
Antaeus: Figure in Greek mythology, one of the Giants, son of Gaia (Earth).. Antaeus challenged all passers-by to wrestling matches and was invincible as long as he remained in contact with his mother, the earth.

Dryads

Dark slender trees
etched against a late gold sky,
I walk among you.

In a triangle of sky framed by branches
hang three faint blue stars, magical in device.
Through this brief fluid moment
stirs an ancient memory
older than flesh . . .
If you would speak,
speak quickly.

Dim voices out of the clustered dark:
    Tell us, tell us of life, tell us of love!
    Here we stand, rooted, bound.
    You who have broken away,
    tell us of life, tell us of love?

Dryad: *In Greek mythology, a female tree spirit.*

Dryads Curious

I know a dryad dwelling in a tree,
A cool and gentle spirit, shadow-eyed,
Who the slow years that creep to set her free
Pent in her patient darkness must abide.
Whispering cypress language that we know,
Italian cypress, slim against the sky,
She waves a sister's greeting as I go;
I breathe the fragrance of her muted sigh.

There is a magic moment when the sun
Dips low and three faint stars hang high above;
I walk among the cypresses, each one
Her green hands reaching toward me as I move,
And, of the older trees, some have begun
To question me of human life and love.

To the Father Tree

Sequoia tree, your life flows deep and chill,
And pulsates slow, to sweeping rhythms stirred;
Anchored in earth, communing with a bird,
Held steadfast by a mightier force than will.
While the high breezes through your branches thrill
Their faint light sings, too distant to be heard,
Your heart unto a mystic silent word
Remotely listening, infinitely still.

Frail human creatures round you wondering creep;
If you can know them, let your quiet heart
From all its centuries spare a moment's grace;
Consider them; they laugh and dance and weep;
In your vast peace grant them a slender part,
These transient children of an alien race.

The Caterpillar

I have crawled long enough upon the ground.
Of all the sustenance I have absorbed
I know there is enough to build my tomb
and weave a silken shroud. Will this material
suffice to make a pair of radiant wings?

The Civilized Rabbit

My grandma lived a fearful life
And ate wild berries in the wood,
But I sit safely in my hutch
And wait until they bring my food.

My lettuce is both fresh and green;
Contentedly I munch away;
My little water pan is filled
Quite regularly once a day.

I should not know which way to turn
If I were set to wander free;
I'm humbly grateful for my lot,
But what would grandma think of me?

After a Thousand Years

A man strokes a cat, and the watching woman
Sees him smile as he never smiles at her
Who has lost, for the dubious honor of being human,
The power to purr.

Freedom

She wore drab colors
and moved sedately
and was concerned with food
for she carried a house on her back.

The house was finely artificed;
it's winding stair especially
admired by the thoughtful;
but she was ill content.

If I could be rid, she said,
of this important house,
I should move freely,
deck my body in rare colors,
and be admired for myself.

So with effort and pain
she rid herself of the house.
Now to view her
is to avert the eyes.

Cat in the Old Village Grocery

He was fat, yellow, handsome,
sleepily amenable to the touch
of any passing customer,
but ruling with dignity
the section of the counter
between the roll of wrapping paper
and the large round cheese.

He never desired to be
a moonlight marauder
and he left no progeny.

I wonder if he ever felt
that he was missing something?

Spring Scenario

Pale discouraged sunlight spent itself
On the drab remains of a dead autumn.
Thick fog and rain closed in
And the stage crew went to work.

When that gray curtain lifted
Acacia billowed gold against a green backdrop
And a flight of white birds
Enlivened the clear sky.

Felines

I am a great blue Persian
with amber eyes.
They call me a cat,
but I have not dealings with my kind
and I do not indulge in kittens.

The man's voice is warm;
his touch sings in my throat.
He lets me couch my plumy length
along his shoulders
and ride above the world.
When he combs my knotted fur
the pain is sweet,
but sometimes I protest aloud
for the joy of speaking
a word he understands.

The woman strokes me
(She is a long-haired one, too,
but her eyes are green, not amber)
and the cat-me purrs to her touch
until I remember
and unsheathe my little daggers;
then she shows her teeth and smiles . . .

I will sharpen my little daggers
for another thousand years.

Couch *(verb)*: *To lay something on a bed or other resting place.*

Old Friends

The kitten stopped in his ecstatic play
And held the pencil briefly in his paws,
Those little, ineffectual, thumbless hands,
And when it fell he looked at me. We shared
The fleeting shadow of a memory.

They had no need of hands, for they were gods,
Housed in great temples, served by humankind
In life, in death and afterward. And I
(Or one of the creatures that have helped to form
That which now bears my name) was proud to be
A servant of the goddess. There was love
Between us, love in strange unhuman form,
The sweeter for a seasoning of fear.

I was the one who feared. Bast sat serene.
If she knew that her rule would disappear
Into the hands of men, perhaps she also
Knew the slow wheel was turning. Who can say
That any domination will endure?
The gods have time for patience; Bast will wait
And wise-eyed kittens purr and flex their claws.

Bast: *Egyptian goddess of protection and cats.*

I Hate Dogs

I hate dogs. They bark. They scratch. They stink.
They maul the tender little kittens, too.
And, more especially when they're young, they think
The world's their fuzzy ball to nip and chew.

I can admire exuberance, in its place;
A dog who has none is a fat old bore;
But I dislike its wet tongue on my face
And when it wrecks my nylons I get sore.

I've known good conversations go to pot
On doggy stories; and I've sat and hated
And squirmed with boredom — who, indeed has not? —
When tales of canine brilliance were related.

So I hate dogs. I know, without contrition,
How anti-social is this frank admission.

California Summer Song

Across the fields, the heavy golden fields
Where toasted grass lies fragrant under June,
Sounds the clear fluting of a lonely bird
Whose random notes make pattern in a tune.

Late falls the day and breathless to its close,
But, song undaunted, shrills the meadow lark:
Fare homeward, traveler, homeward to your nest;
Soon comes the dark -- soon comes the dark.

From a Car Window

Sagebrush eruptions
   scaling dry hills;
   small useless trees,
   falsely, desperately green;
   tormented palms
   grotesquely limbed.
A stray cabin squats
   flatly in the gasping heat.
Does a woman live there,
   or only a man?

Acacia: *Tree or shrub of warm climates that bears clusters of yellow or white flowers.*

The Suppliant

I thrust a fishhook through a grasshopper
who beat the air with desperate hands and prayed
unto his god. I made him more secure
and lightly flicked him into a shallow stream.
A cautious trout rose, nibbled, turned away;
I swore a bit; the punctured insect drifted
downstream, no doubt still praying to his god.

Ants

The ant colony was starving.
One day a scout returned
with a report of food
at the end of a long dangerous journey.
They braved the unfamiliar ascent
in the outer wall of my house
and entered through an electric outlet

I called the exterminator;
he came promptly, and I was left in peace.
But I could almost have wept
for such small creatures,
so brave, so resourceful
and so doomed.

Suppliant: *A person making a humble plea to someone in power or authority.*

Self-Restraint in April

I would not go to buy a house
in April, in the countryside,
although my eyes turn longingly
to look and covet as I ride.

For periwinkle, pimpernel,
green moss along a picket fence
and sagging eaves weighed down with vines
can overthrow my common sense.

And whitewash is as beautiful
as paint and stucco to the eye
when fields are verdant all about
and cleanly azure is the sky.

I know the things a house must have
to make it what it ought to be.
but strangely I forget them all
for one gnarled blooming apple tree.

A well kept garden has its charm,
but what a pure, peculiar thrill
to spy, by some forsaken door,
a lone, persistent daffodil.

So, till I've wealth to throw away
I'11 look and covet as I ride,
but I will never buy a house
in April, in the countryside.

Dust Thou Art

As I went barefoot in a country lane
the deep soft dust curled up between my toes;
the chaparral was dry, the oaks were still;
in the siesta hour I walked alone,
as innocent as an untouched guitar.

The summer ended gently; early rain
dimpled the dust, and such a fragrance breathed
as made me leap and run and spread my arms,
responding to a joy as old as time
when a sweet Breath imparted life to dust.

Chaparral: *A dense, impenetrable thicket of shrubs or dwarf trees (from the Spanish word for an evergreen oak shrub land).*

Prelude

Out in the hedgerow at the break of day
A gray bird perches; from his throat there streams
An endless four note song, as if he deems
A fifth would mar the sweetness of his lay.
I have a lute with four worn strings, these themes
In endless repetition I must play,
Strive to vary their measure as I may,
Music and darkness, love and baffled dreams.

In autumn, when the ripening of the fruit
Brings back the singer, each familiar note
Tuned to the pattern of a gray bird's throat,
Awakes an answering echo in my lute.
Each autumn sees that winter less remote
When, one string breaking, all the rest fall mute.

La Noche

I love the grand sweep of the wide spreading dark.
    Its audible silence, its visible space,
Its cool freshening breeze from the beautiful sea
    That kisses my fevered face.

The day is so long and so dull or so gay
    (For the rising sun drives away the rest)
That I feel when I gaze on the indigo sky
    That on night's ample motherly breast
I can lean for relief from the cares of my life;
    For the winds through the pine branches sigh,
And their soft alto notes with the sea's far off bass
    Croon a natural lullaby.

But the day with its bustling importunate life,
    Forbids night's restful sway hold for long,
And as first faintly blushes the eastern sky
    Lo, the soul of the darkness is gone.

An Unusual Honor

Separated from his migrating flock
a great Canada goose
alighted on the march
and made his way to my open door.
He stood there with dignity
and in some way made known his need.
I held out to him what food I had
and he ate delicately from my hand
several squares of baked squash.
Satisfied, he walked away.
At the edge of the grass he faced me,
spread his great wings wide
bowed his shining head
then turned and soared into the sky.

Unfriendly Skies

(December 28, 1976)

The sky remains inexorably blue,
Or dull with haze of gray lugubrious hue,
While stunted grass and thirsty birds complain
to clouds that have forgotten how to rain.

(P.S. December 29. Today it rained.)

Inexorably: *in a way that is impossible to stop or prevent.*
Lugubrious: *Looking or sounding sad or dismal.*

9
MOCK US GENTLY

Mock Us Gently

After dinner some of us gather
for a dish of talk.
Our tongues are livelier than our ears
but we manage to gather material
for a bit of kindly gossip.

We do not linger late,
bid one another a cheery goodnight,
knowing there will probably be a morrow,
but if not—well, anyhow,
goodnight.

Overheard

A proper little couple,
septuagenarians both,
walked happily arm in arm
down an almost empty hall.
"Did you hear her?" asked the wife.
"She said I have pretty legs."
"And so you have, my dear,"
he responded gallantly,
"but she doesn't know what's between them."

Flattery Will Get You

Whatever I was playing,
Clift always asked for *Lara's Song*.
Tonight I had chosen Scottish tunes
for the dinner music.
I saw him leave his place
and start for the piano.
I know what he's going to say,
I thought resentfully,
and I won't do it.
He approached the piano,
laid his arm across my shoulders, saying,
"You're a sweetheart and I love you,"
and returned to his table.
I finished *Loch Lomond*
and what do you think I played next?

Lara's Song: *Also known as "Lara's Theme," as a light motif developed for the character Lara in the movie Doctor Zhivago (1965). It was the basis of the song "Somewhere, My Love" which was nominated for the Grammy Award for Song of the Year in 1967 (it lost).*
Loch Lomond: *"The Bonnie Banks o' Loch Lomond" is a well-known Scottish song first published in 1841. The first lines of the chorus are, "You take the high road and I'll take the low road, and I'll be in Scotland a'fore ye."*

One of Life's Moments

A fat old gentleman
walked heavily down a carpeted corridor,
empty before him.
Close behind, a lady,
in no hurry to pass his bulk form,
moved silently as a ghost.

Suddenly he stopped,
grasped the handrail with both hands,
and, with face to the wall,
emitted a long, loud blast of wind.

In a split second the lady's mind
presented three alternatives:
a nonchalant, well-bred "Good afternoon,"
or an absurd "I beg your pardon,"
or "I'm stone deaf—didn't hear a thing."

But he was slow to turn his head
and she was able to slip past
and continue her dignified progress
without confrontation.

Blast of wind: *A fart.*

Two Big Words

We know what small-talk is,
for most of our talk is very small indeed:
Did you have a good lunch?
The doctor wants me to ...
I don't like this windy weather.

But it will not be long
before two proud words
rise above the small talk,
"My daughter. ..."

Our Grandchildren

Two feckless young lovers
pooled their meager funds
to buy a water bed.
They could not look ahead
to the breaking of bonds
from which youth recovers
—but not a water bed.

You and I Were Young, Maggie

Often, in the evening,
I play old songs for half an hour.

Riding in wheel chairs,
leaning on canes,
or walking carefully
on fairly steady feet,
they come around the piano and sing.
These are the lucky ones
who keep a cheerful face and a tuneful heart.

The Wheel Chair

To some it is a friend,
a refuge, a shelter;
to some, an ignominious prison.
There is one old lady
who holds her handsome head erect
and sits as if on a throne;
covering, with some gallantry,
a sad, frightened little girl.

When You and I Were Young, Maggie: *A famous folk and popular song, first written as a poem by George Johnson in 1864 and then set to music by James Austin Butterfield. It has been covered by many artists, including Gene Autry, Perry Como, Benny Goodman, Fats Waller, and it was a 1951 hit for Bing Crosby.*

One Answer

They came here together,
lifelong companions,
May and her grand Steinway.

Her hands were still dexterous on the keys
but memory was fraying.
One day, on the fourth bar
of a Beethoven presto,
the last strand broke.

May arose, white and trembling,
and tottered to her room.
From that day on she refused to eat.

In a few weeks
the frail body released her.
She left us her piano
and the memory of her dignity and courage.

Presto: *A fast-paced piece of music.*

I Was Privileged

The organ and I played cheerful tunes.
We had three listeners:
One was a small, tired woman,
Full of pain and sorrow.

Change the music, came into my mind,
And the *Brahms Lullaby* came into my fingers,
Then *Lead Kindly Light*.

The small, tired woman went to sleep
And did not waken.

I thanked the guardian spirit
That I had heard and heeded
The whisper of that gentle passing.

Brahms' Lullaby: *Traditional children's lullaby, written by Johannes Brahms in 1868. The common English version starts with the line, "Lullaby and good night."*
Lead Kindly Light: *A very well known hymn, written by John Henry Newman in 1833 as a poem.*

Fondly Remembered

Two women stood, heads together
in earnest conversation.
In passing them I did not slacken pace,
being unwilling to intrude
on a serious private matter.
So all I heard was,
"He'd have an egg.
Sometimes he'd have a scrambled egg.
Oh, he was a fine man."

Channel 5

Nelly is ninety-three.
One knows at a glance
that life has petted her
as it sometimes does pet
a pretty little woman.
Saturday evening she arrived at the table
dressed in pink, wearing her pearls.
"Going out?" we asked. She smiled.
"No, but Lawrence comes on at eight;
he might ask me to dance."

Lawrence Welk: *American musician and band leader who hosted "The Lawrence Welk Show" from 1951-1982. First on the radio (1951-1955) and then on television (1955-1982), the show was known for Welk's personable style, "champagne music," featuring bubbles and focused on conservative renditions of popular music, show tunes, polkas and novelty songs.*

Music Critic

The Dixieland Jazz Band,
twenty beautiful young people,
came with a kindly intention
and gave us a concert.

Listening from a distance,
I thought the sparse applause indicated
that the generation gap
was yawning.

I asked one of the grandmas how she liked the music.
"Well," she said sweetly, "it is better
than to be on the street with guns
killing people."

The Whisper

She stops me in the hall,
puts her small pale mouth
close to my ear and whispers,
with a cold breath, of a thing
that happened long ago in her grey life.

When she receives that tap on the shoulder
which we all await,
will she, I wonder, continue
to whisper along the halls,
unaware of change?

Don't Feed the Pigeons

Sleek, iridescent,
noisy, greedy, quarrelsome,
they assembled at my door
for the word had got around
that grain appeared there at six o'clock.
One fat handsome bully,
who had a wife and concubine,
kept the pecking order
firmly established.
They put on a floor show for me every evening.

Dialog with a Strawberry

I said to a giant strawberry,
"You are man's error, not nature's.
To be merely handsome is not
your proper duty. Honest strawberries
perfume the air with their aroma,
saturate shortcake with generous juice.
Are you not ashamed
to be so coarse, dry, tasteless?"

The bloated thing on the plate
gave back my stare.
"You bought me," it said,
"Now let's take a look at you."

Incident in a Low Key

A strange lady held out a thin hand.
I took it and she said, or so I thought,
"I've lost my mind and I don't know where to find it."
I replied facetiously, "Have you advertised?"
She brushed that off and went on talking
until I gathered
that it was her nightgown that was lost.
I suggested the Lost and Found.
She made a soft noise that might have been thank you.
We moved in opposite directions,
each carrying a small bewilderment.

The Sinner

An old lady sat at a table,
cheating at solitaire.
A stranger paused to watch.
An angel took down both names.

"You're cheating," said the stranger.
"It's my game, I'll play it as I like,"
said the old lady.

The stranger shrugged contemptuously
as he turned away.
The angel made a black mark
against one of the names.

Violet

She is a small strong-fibered Englishwoman,
never a wife; the man she would have loved
died in the Boer War. They never met.
She made herself a family, of birds
and plants and children and small animals
and books, and all mankind. Nearly a century
lies now upon her shoulders. She is tired.
Her eyes, her once skilled hands, even her wit,
it seems to her, are failing. Several times
the body sought release, but every time
the doctors brought it back. She acquiesced
and faced the weariness as best she could,
with ill concealed impatience to be gone,
to spread her wings and find her youth again.

Boer War: *Usually refers to the Second Boer War (1899 - 1902) which was fought between the United Kingdom and the two Boer states, the South African Republic (Transvaal Republic) and the Orange Free State.*

Call Me Buck

"Call me Buck," he says.
"My parents named me Audley;
How could they do that
To a poor little kid?"

Buck is six foot three
And weighs, maybe,
A hundred and forty soakin'-wet.
He wears bib overalls
And a sombrero.
He knows how to talk to mules,
But in polite conversation
He uses only ordinary cuss words.
His room is a workshop
Where he makes elegant toys.

The only song he requests
Is *Moonlight and Roses*.

Moonlight and Roses: *Country-style love song written by Ben Black, Edwin LeMare and Neil Moret, It was made popular by Jim Reeves, featured on the album Moonlight and Roses which reached #1 on the US country charts in 1964.*

We Entertained Royalty

He strolled past my open door,
a regal white Persian.
When I said, "kitty-kitty,"
he gave me a cold shoulder
and a twitch of his plume;
I knew I had made a faux pas.
The next time he appeared
I said, "Your Majesty";
he paused and looked at me.

Three of us, occupying adjacent rooms
on the side facing the marsh
gradually won him from his feline caution.
He entered at our doors,
lay on our cushions,
and trusted us to guard his sleep
when he rested after hunting.
We fed him bits of meat
filched from our own dinner
until he grew fat, and too pernickety
to accept meat loaf.

The conspiracy lasted quite a while
but the powers that be
could not wink forever,
and a home was found for His Majesty.
Now three lonely women
have another small memory to cherish.

pernickety: *British term for persnickety; fussy, difficult to please.*

10

AGING, DEATH & GOD

Vision Before Choice

To be born is to enter
    with determination
    through a narrow gate
    a cold uncertain world.

To survive is to be
    shrewd to gain protection
    strong to forgo inaction
    industrious to breathe

To die, is it
    to tune the will
    to release certain bonds
    and sink into waiting hands?

Squandered

She cannot raise remembrance as she would,
And knows she will not savor love again
As in those first ecstatic moments when
She tasted it and found that it was good.
Painted on fire, sculptured in live blood,
Etched on a dream in silver, many men
Have taken amorous portraiture since then;
His face is blurred and dimly understood.

She gazes coldly in her looking-glass
And notices the wrinkles at her eyes.
Another futile day has come and gone.
Encouragingly, life is sure to pass.
She lifts dramatic arms toward the skies
And holds them there ten seconds in a yawn.

Silence

I have lain in the dark
and listened
to the thin, high shrilling
of the blood in my veins,
and I have wondered
what pure silence is.

Sometime I shall know pure silence
Not blurred by the clamor of flesh.
Shall I know how to bear it?

Immortality

If ancient dreams of floating through the air
on angel wings upborne; if all my fond
and yearning hopes for friends, who passed beyond
the door of death before me, prove to share
the fate of all mirage; if waiting there
is nothing but the fathomless black pond
of non-existence, what shall be my prayer?

The future failing, cherish the glorious past,
when out of bloody suffering, toil and tears,
man finds his hands, and looks into the sky,
and struggles into speech, and at long last
inquires for truth and shrugs away false fears —
I think I can be satisfied to die.

Apropos of Roses

I know I shall not live to be inured
To certain flowers, too rich to be endured;
The creamy bowl of a magnolia bell,
Brimming with sorcery craftily matured
Through days of slow warm ripening, in each cell
Of pointed bud, secretly to compel
Attentive sunshine, heavily redolent
Of foreign spices, wild, incredible.

When in the darkness, wide-flung, passion-spent,
Lax petals droop, too weary to bear scent,
Flower of a lost young world, your paleness
Outs its nostalgia to the firmament,
Plead with the moon, white lips, for her unclose
I will escape you with a small red rose.

When One Book Closes

Of strong faith in the soul's surviving
I do not yield one jot or tittle
because, in these brief years of living
I've learned so much -- and know so little.

When all the world pronounce me dead,
this vehicle to dust returning,
may I be one of whom it's said:
She learned, and will continue learning.

A Prayer

Thou who art wise, lay silence on my lips
until the word of wisdom shall be plain.
Thou who art strong, pervade my hands with grace
to touch with skill or patiently refrain.
Thou whose white standard I aspire to bear,
hold thy perfection mirrored to my eyes;
so shall my feet prove steady on the path
that leads to thee, the strong, the true, the wise.

Cameos

Out of my living red stone,
out of my dead white,
I have carved a few
small neat cameos.

Stone is a shapeless thing,
a fragile perishable thing,
so I who would endure
take the pattern of cameos.

The fine accurate chisel
is deliberate, sure of stroke;
and I, hand and stone and chisel,
cry aloud in the shaping:

Laggard, laggard is that quiet day
when I shall be all cameos!

Old Rose

A little whitewashed house
nestled under two giant oaks
surrounded by the rolling acres
of a foothill vineyard.
There was no garden
but someone had planted a Spanish rose bush
whose small flowers, packed with petals
carried the scent of all roses
since the garden of Eden.

Ignoring the old-fashioned rose,
the grown-ups made a fence
and planted a plot to their liking.
For ten important years
this place was my childhood home.

I saw it again, long afterward.
The little house, the giant trees were gone
The vineyard had been destroyed,
the land torn up by a dredger for gold.
There was no trace of our planting
only the stubborn Spanish rose
put forth a flower
with all the ancient fragrance.

The Body Speaks

Are you ashamed of these distorted hands
that once were strong and beautiful; this flesh,
So faded and so feeble, which was once
Firm and resilient, able to perform
The tasks your vagrant will has laid upon it?

Let no resentment, no hostility
Express itself in pain. The time draws near
I shall be scattered to the open winds
And you will travel where I cannot follow.
Let these long years of mutual service end
In mutual forgiveness and release.

I Am
What I Am
When I Am

I learn, as I draw nearer to the source
of my endowment and my limitation
to look on my mistakes without remorse
and view my victories without elation.

My Town

I am homesick for a town I have not seen
Where pleasant hilltops sing against the sky
In lilting lines of patterned melody,
And trees new sprung in luminous startling green,
Direct and cleanly perpendicular
Fling from the soil their penetrating line
And clear unheated light is sifted fine
Through all the mild and gentle atmosphere.

I know its pools of blue-eyed flowers, its grass
Resilient in every springing blade,
The homely roofs, the comfortable, clean
Old cottages where peaceful folk may pass
Unhastened lives. I shall, I am afraid,
Die homesick for a town I have not seen.

If I Will

Silky meadows purr like great cats
under the stroking of the wind;
pale shells of the quince blossoms
nestle under motherly gray leaves;
and I am free to go, if I will,
where gay music
crashes under light,
or where campfires
pack into comfortable coals
beneath dark trees.

Houses

All my life I have been a builder of houses,
rooms accurately measured,
doors and windows fitted,
carpets and curtains chosen,
pantry and ice-box filled.

I have built enough houses to line a long street.
No one has ever lived in a house of my building.
Sometime I shall take up my abode
where they await me.

In that country there is room
for each to stand, withdrawn
among its own trees,
far from its own gates.

One after another, unhurried,
I shall live in them,
lying on each hearth-rug
with the one for whom that house was built,
renewing acquaintance with past selves
through desires made visible.

Then, it may be, at last,
satisfied with houses,
I shall set out alone
on a leisurely tour
among the planets.

A Long View

The past returns to me in bits and pieces;
I don't remember everything at once;
Sometimes I think of nephews or of nieces;
Or blush for times I acted like a dunce.
And roadside scenes come over me in flashes
Inopportune to anything I do;
A campfire—pouring water on the ashes—
A ride in the rain beside the current "you."
An orchard where myrobolana ran wild;
A dog or cat who was a special friend;
A little book I handled as a child;
The pictures crowd and cluster toward the end.
And so the old, with absent-gazing eyes,
Withdraw and listen to their memories.

Myrobolana: *A small plum, also called Cherry Plum, with edible fruit but also used as a garden ornamental.*

As It Might Happen

Scene 1, The Beyond

First Spirit: Friend, will you do my work for me today?

Second Spirit: Of course, and gladly, as you would do for me.

First Spirit: You do not question me, but I will tell you.
   One who was once my daughter will be born
   Into this life. You know how they expect
   To see their mothers' faces when they wake.

Second Spirit: How will it be, do you think, an easy birth?

First Spirit: I mean that this awakening shall be different
   From any she has known for years, poor soul!
   Of late, you may have noticed, I've withdrawn
   At times from all our happy mingled tasks
   For a preoccupation of my own
   That must be solitary. I was building
   A house.

Second Spirit: You — building a house? But what have you
   To do with houses?

First Spirit: Only what we all
   Must do with things that cling to human hearts.
   She loved a house once, one of the few loves
   That did not come to sorrow. She shall wake
   In a soft bed with lavender scented sheets
   And a pink and blue log-cabin patchwork quilt;
   The paper on the walls — I had to search
   My memory for that paper — has a silly
   Little design of roses and carnations;

> At the window — this is most important —
> The shadow of green vine leaves shall flow in
> And tremble on the wall before her eyes.

Second Spirit: I see you have enjoyed this preparation
> As much, perhaps, as you did once before.

First Spirit: Perhaps I have; you smile at me so kindly
> That I am moved to smiling at myself,
> And she, too, will smile with us when she knows,
> But not when she first wakes. When they have lived
> As she has lived it takes a little time
> Before they can be whole and free again.

Second Spirit: Your house has other rooms?

First Spirit: Oh, yes, a kitchen!
> A beautiful kitchen with a good wood stove —
> You should have seen me blackening it — the fire
> Shines through the open places under the grate
> And dances on the wall of evenings. Then
> There's the yellow light of a squat coal oil lamp
> That stands upon the checkered tablecloth
> Of red and white; and on the shelf are dishes
> All somewhat nicked — there's one old mustache cup
> I didn't even know that I remembered.

Second Spirit: What treasures lie in the mine of memory!

First Spirit: I know it's funny. And you have permission
> To be even more amused at my next find.
> Curled up on a shabby cushion on the seat
> Of a creaky, sidewise-traveling rocking chair —

Second Spirit: A cat?

First Spirit: The cat! old orange-tawny Tom
   Tough and adventurous, with one ear chewed off.
   It's seldom that he condescends to purr
   But when he feels her hand I think he will.

First Spirit: Sometime I'd like to see your little house,
   The cat, the patchwork quilt, the fine black stove.
   It isn't often we derive so much
   Pleasure as this from helping them get born.

Scene II, The County Hospital

First Nurse: This one's about gone, just a matter of
   A few more minutes. Nothing we can do.
   There hasn't been since first they brought her in.
   Don't leave her now.

Second Nurse: She's going easily.
   I'm always glad when they don't make a fight.
   I think she's gone already — no — what is it?

First Nurse: What was it she said?

Second Nurse: Nothing that made sense. And anyhow
   There's nobody to care for what she said.
   It sounded like "The vine leaves at the window…"

Moving Day (Inventory)

I am about to move out of this house
into one of my father's mansions.
Which of my possessions
would I, if I could, take with me?

Some things I have inherited,
and these are so much a part of me
that I cannot know
whether they are trash or treasure.

Some small gifts from friends
are made golden by love;
but for what I bought at a high price
I accept the loss,
taking with me the lesson.

Some precious things
are too shabby for a mansion;
but surely there will be a small room
where I can place a rocking-chair
and hand a framed cross-stitch motto:
God Bless Our Home.

Bronze Chrysanthemums

Brown flowers for the soul that sets forth in November,
finished and tranquil, licensed to evade
the yuletide joyance that has nearly made
his loneliness a torment to remember.
She will escape holly and mistletoe,
having survived the summer and the rose;
in that uncertain garden where she goes
what flowers may burgeon, what perfumes may blow?

When all my life has slanted up to death
and I, arriving breathless, pause to rest,
when that which I await at long length comes
and kind hands fashion me a farewell wreath,
let one who loves me lay on my quiet breast
gaillardias and bronze chrysanthemums.

Gaillardia: *Common name for blanket flower, a flower plant in the sunflower family, native to North and South America. Comes in almost any shade of yellow, orange, red, purplish, brown, white or multi-colored. Blooms in the late spring until first frost.*
Chrysanthemums: *Garden flowers (native to Asia) with showy blooms in many colors, shapes and sizes. They bloom from late summer into the fall.*

A Hope

I've trembled before judgment. As a child
I never doubted that the Angel's book
With every rebel thought and angry look
And selfish word, was accurately compiled
In pages of black record, to be filed
Card-indexed in the S's. And I took
Small comfort in the timid hope that luck
Would see me through - God was not meek and mild!

Since having children of my own, I've had
This notion - He may scan the shame and doubt
And folly under my name, then smile and say:
There, there, my child, you weren't so very bad;
Later we'll let you work the payment out.
Just now - run out in the grass a while and play!

Heaven

I live alone. A mighty barrier
Between myself and my friend's self is raised;
Two bodies intervene between two souls.
But looking each into the other's eyes
We catch a glimpse of something beautiful --
Perfection striving to express itself
Through imperfections -- and a vague thought comes.
That when this hidden beauty grows too grand
To be imprisoned more and is set free
To manifest itself, that must be heaven.

I strive alone. I tread a weary path,
And often in despair stretch out my hands
Calling upon the darkness for a Friend,
But no one answers. And my heart grows faint,
My courage falters, for I can ask in dread,
"To what avail do I attain the height
Of my desire, if when the height be reached
I stand alone?" But something drives me on,
And lonely, fearing, yearning, still I climb.
At last the height is reached, and -- joy of joys! --
I see awaiting me with outstretched hands,
The Friends whom I have longed for. And they smile,
"We too climbed up alone. It is a way
Which each must tread himself, for none can help.
Each knew not that the others struggled too,
But now we know -- even as we are known"

The Teacher

Passing through this world like a flame,
I have warmed
I have illuminated
I have seared.

Tell me, before I flicker into darkness
is there somewhere a torch
that I have kindled?

Departure

Then I shall walk an avenue of peace
Straight from a mountain over a level cloud
That fills the valley; and I shall release
My gaze into a setting sun bright-browed
With silver; feel the flow of evening wind
Along my arms, the kiss of solitude
Upon these faithful lips; and night shall find
My eager soul magnificently nude.

There will be silence, and the exquisite cool
Ash of the ether parting to let me through;
There may be strange reflections in the pool
Of stars, but I shall stroll along the blue,
Unweighted, free, accepting well-content
The hospitality of the firmament.

11

HUMOR & WORDPLAY

Jealous Doggy-Rel

The elegant Mrs. Van Twitter
Admired a St. Bernard's litter
    When she tried to appease
    Her irate Pekinese
The son of a bitch up and bit her.

Jymn's Hymn

A pious old toper was Jymn;
When he started to pour out a hymn
    In rhyme and in rhythm
    We all joined in wythm
Because we were all full to the brymn.

Short Story

He said, without any preamble,
"I think I will just take a ramble."
    At the end of the journey
    He woke on a gurney
In a hospital ward in Istamble.

Doggerel: *Poetry that is irregular in rhythm and rhyme, often deliberately for comic effect.*
Toper: *A hard drinker or chronic drunkard.*
Preamble: *An introduction to a speech or story.*

Stately Names of England

PEPYS (pronounced "Peeps")

A lady who met Samuel Pepys
Declared that he gave her the crepys
    But when he had kissed her
    He coolly dismissed her
and now she just sits there and wepys.

KNOLLYS ("Noles")

    A girl of the family of Knollys
    Was well trained in acrobat rollys
        But she shocked the grandstand
        When she did a handstand
    For her panty hose were full of hollys.

BEAULIEU ("Bewley")

There was a young matron of Beaulieu
Whose children were rude and unreaulieu
    When they were dismissed
    with a pat on the wrist
She thought they were punished undeaulieu

WRIOTHESLEY ("Risley")

A lady named Hepzibah Wriothesley
Was attacked by a very large griothesley.
    She took such a fright
    That her hair turned white
and became all curly and friothesley.

WORCHESTER ("Wooster")
GLOUCHESTER ("Gloster")
and LEICESTER ("Lester")

There once was a frisky young jeicester
Whose sole aim in life was to peicester
    With trick and with jolk
    He bedeviled the folk
Of Worcestershire, Glouchester and Leicester.

BEAUCHAMP ("Beecham")
and CHOLMONDELEY ("Chumly")

Prof Beauchamp inquired of Prof Cholmondeley,
"Why look at your students so glomondeley?"
    Said Cholmondeley to Beauchamp,
    "Because I can't teauchamp;
They just sit and stare at me dolmondeley."

Re-Verse

Oh, pray don't ask me, "Yow are hoo?"
I grine and whumble all day long;
this weanter wither gets me down
And everything woes grong.

I swear my weaters all to rags
With tutting on and paking off;
I steat and swifle when I'm warm,
When cold I keeze and snough.

Young Hero

Three touchdowns snatch a victory from defeat;
No future triumph can be half so sweet.
He will receive, ere this brief glory fades,
Emoluments, encomiums, accolades.

Emoluments: *A salary, fee or profit from employment or activity.*
Encomiums: *A speech or piece of writing that praises someone or something highly.*
Accolades: *An award or privilege granted as a special honor or as an acknowledgment of merit; An expression of praise or admiration.*

Pippa Passes

Mr. Browning sat at his desk, for once in a placid mood.
"The year's at spring," he said, and felt that the line was good.
What next? Why, "Day's at the morn;" and then he glanced at the clock;
"Morning's at seven" he observed. It was time for his morning walk.
It was really a lovely day, with dew all over the grass
(But that's prose) "The hillside's dew-pearled,"
      Now there's a line that will pass.

So he had four good lines; he had better begin to rhyme.
Spring, bring, thing, wing, he mused. He almost had it that time.
"The lark's on the wing," of course. Now let's get down to earth —
And find a rhyme for morn. scorn, torn, born surely no dearth —
His foot scrunched on a snail. "The snail's on the thorn," he said
He was very pleased with himself and smiled and nodded his head.

"Pippa Passes": *A verse drama by Robert Browning, published in 1841, a well known passage of which is:*

> *The year's at the spring,*
> *And day's at the morn;*
> *Morning's at seven;*
> *The hill-side's dew-pearled;*
> *The lark's on the wing;*
> *The snail's on the thorn;*
> *God's in His heaven—*
> *All's right with the world!*

Surrealist Trilogy

The Fur Cup

Decipherably he lies in bed
Wearing a saucepan on his head
Full two two sizes too too large
And wreathed about his name
Twice fifty mighty tongues did barge
Into the candle flame.

Cold nuances of forked steel
Unprepossessing as to heel
And frankly ovoid as to lurch
Rolled down his purple throat
While he whom no extremes could smirch
Lay pallid and remote.

Till all the mountains shall fold up
Still I will lay a buttercup
Fiercely upon his counterpane
And smoulder chastely on
Till all the seas shall smell of rain
And utterly be gone.

Surrealist: *The principle, ideal or practice of producing fantastic or incongruous imagery or effects in art, literature, film, or theater by means of unnatural or irrational juxtapositions and combinations.*

The Fur Saucer

I used up all the nonchalance I had
Remembering how that last blue fragment went.
Who dares to tell me what he thought I meant?
Suspense — and then — suspenders, which is bad.
Carefully seedy, delicately mad,
The house I sought, pervaded by the scent
Of morbid green unease, more evident
Than verminous paraphrases all unclad.
Exact and scandalous she crept away
Down the long ribbon dangling at her waist;
The kitchen sink remains a compromise
Whose sole mobility is in the sway
Of armatures ill-wound in frantic haste;
But holocausts are rarely so precise.

The Fur Spoon

This is a challenge, I perceive,
To rub a faintly molded sleeve
Across an eager nose,
While heroes and canaries cry
And calm spittoons in slumber lie
And solemn smacks offend the eye
From these and eke from those.
No lily or no frenzied slug
Shall mar the coolness of our rug
Except we grab it loose;
But gently, gently shall we keep
The sad profusion of our sleep
Until the Cappadocian Peep
At last proclaim its use.

Cappadocian Peep: *May reference the tiny windows ("peep holes") in the cone-shaped dwellings built somewhere around 1800 BC in Cappadocia, a region in central Turkey.*

Geography and Poetry*

Coffee from the Orinoco
Is not so good for us as cocoa.

Diamonds, taken from the ground,
In Brazil are chiefly found.

Tallow, in the Argentine,
Makes light so things can be seen.

India rubber from the trees
Erases pencil marks with ease.

Silver and copper in the Andes
Come to us and go for candies.

Peruvian bark is good for chills,
Fever and for other ills.

Guano on the coast is found,
With which to fertilize the ground.

In Paraguay is found the tea
For my grandma, but not for me.

In Columbia is indigo,
Which is a dye that all must know.

Pampas on the plains does grow,
for the cows to eat, you know.

Co-authored by Sibyl and an unnamed friend in 1899 (age 11)

Valentine Verses

Ah, lovely, blooming Miss McRae,
Thousand times fairer than the day!
May I but join the loving band
Of beaux whose rings are on your hand?
For all your love I dare not hope.
(Yet I use Cuticura soap
As beautifier. It is said
'Twill grow a new face on one's head,
A face of fair and sweet expression.)
But pardon me for this digression.
I started in to write this note
(Have patience, it is nearly wrote)
To say I'll be your faithful spaniel
If I but may,
      Your own,
           Jim Daniel

      Ah, dear Leona, how sad if
      fond lovers ever have a tiff;
      You know my love for you is true,
      Though off the handle once I flew;
      Darling, no peace can e'er be mine,
      Till you're again my valentine.
      On Christmas night you looked so fair old
      Love revived in the heart of Harold.

Dear Anna,
My passion clamors to be heard,
If only in a single word.
And at this time of lovers true
I fain would pay my vows to you;
Fond thoughts within my bosom lie,
Which I'd express if not too shy.
Come weal, come woe, come rain or shine,
You are my only valentine.
Pray think of this when with Jack you ride
For this from your loving, jealous,
            Clyde

      Dear Amy,
           If you'll heed my signs
      Because you are so awful nice.
      "Ve" heart when from despair you'll save is
      "Vat" of
          Chester Thomas Davis

11

WOMEN OF THE BIBLE

The Story of Cain
as Told By His Wife

He wandered to our campfire, and the men
took up their spears to kill him, for they saw
he was a stranger, and no outlander
might walk upon our ground and live. He spoke.
"Kill me," he said, "if you can, for I am weary
of wandering, hunger, cold and loneliness.
I have known many fears, but not the fear
of death; this sign protects me from your weapons."
He pushed the shaggy hair from his brow; the men
saw what was stamped there and they were afraid.
"I only ask," he said, "to lie for a night
beside your fire; then I will go away."
They asked his name and kindred, and he wept.
"I have no kindred. You may call me Cain."

When morning came he rose to go away.
We offered him fresh meat, but he refused,
saying he had never eaten flesh. He would seek
herbs and the fruit of the forest. But the men
were loath to let him go for he had told
great tales beside the campfire. "Stay with us,"
they said, "and we will teach you how to wield
the spear and kill your meat; and you shall tell
your stories from the West, the land of fire."
"There is no land of fire," he said. "The glow
that shines so red in the clouds at the end of day

The Story of Cain as Told By His Wife

is the reflection of a burning sword
that turns and twists within the angel's hand
who guards the eastern gate of Paradise.
That, too, is far to the west of that good land
which once I called my -- home." When his voice broke
on that last word, a heavy silence fell.

We could not understand this sadness; surely
our home is where we pitch the tents; our land
is where we hunt. When it is time to leave
we seek another hunting ground and go
without a backward glance, much less a tear.
"Why did you leave your land?" the Old Man asked.
"God drove me out. I had offended him."
Then, seeing all the questions in their eyes,
Cain set himself to tell the bitter tale.

"My father Adam, he who named all things
that walk or fly or swim, had heard the Lord
asking an offering. My brother Abel
and I must choose the thing we valued most
and give it to the Lord. We built an altar
of polished stones laid smoothly with great care
and all the skill we knew. Each then prepared
his gift, not knowing what would please the Lord,
but giving of our best. I made a mound
of pomegranates, grapes and figs, surrounded
with artfully woven sheaves of grain and flowers.
It was so beautiful that I was sure
he must be pleased, not only with his fruits

The Story of Cain as Told By His Wife

but with my skill. I set it on the altar
where Abel's offering lay, a small white lamb
dead in its blood. When the Lord's voice spoke
that was the offering he received with pleasure,
ignoring mine. I was so sorely hurt
I could not hide my bitter disappointment
and faced the Lord in anger. He rebuked me
and sent me forth. My brother stood there smiling."

The tale is now familiar. Our men,
hearing it for the first time, thought it wrong
that Cain should kill his brother for a smile;
his exile well deserved; but they also knew
how broken pride can goad a man to murder.
His punishment was no concern of ours,
and he had charmed us with his power of speech.
They bade him choose a wife and join the tribe.

I am the wife he chose, and I was glad
for he was strong and fair. I gave him sons
and daughters while the bearing years were mine.
And afterward the children's children came
to swell the tribe; until when we were old
we had lost count, but some of them we knew.

When it was time to move we found a land
still farther east. The hunting there was good
and there was also rich and fertile ground.
The curse still followed Cain. He could not plant
the seed or till the soil to good effect
but he could teach others. Our young men
began to learn of him how to grow crops

The Story of Cain as Told By His Wife

and live a settled life from year to year.
His hands had wisdom of their own to work
in wood and stone. He built a house for me,
and gradually a city grew around us.

Though not now wandering, Cain was still, in his heart,
a fugitive, forever yearning back
to his lost home and his lost Lord. A deep
perplexity haunted him. He understood
his punishment for murder; that was just;
but why had the Lord refused his offering
of fruit and flowers so artfully displayed?
"My punishment is more than I can bear,"
he said at first; but he had learned to bear it.
It was the other thing which haunted him,
the cruel doubt, the everlasting "Why?"

"Who is this Lord who ruled the western land?"
I asked of Cain. "Is he as fair as you?"
"No man has seen his face, not even Adam,
who walked with him in the garden, for they talked
only in darkness, in the cool of evening.
His voice is like a thunder in the heart."
Cain paused; he was remembering that voice;
and I was silent, noting how the shade
lay strongly on him, setting him apart
from careless men and trivial occupations.
The Shadow lightened only when his hands
were busy with some craft, creating beauty.

The Story of Cain as Told By His Wife

He lived to be the Old Man of the tribe
and many sought his counsel, which he gave
as best he could, in all humility.
And children to the seventh generation,
now numbered by the hundreds, called me mother.
They often brought us little gifts, wild flowers
or fruit, or things their childish hands had made,
which Cain received with smiling gratitude
and sadness in the smile, for he still saw
in memory an altar where his own
gift lay unregarded. But with age
he had achieved a measure of content,
and love of children can heal many wounds.

We sat together at the close of day,
not speaking, for our long companionship
had so attuned our minds there was no need.
We faced the west. The glory of the sword
was very bright. I looked into his face
and saw a change; the mark of deathlessness
had faded from his brow. I held his hand
till it grew cold in mine. I was alone.
I think the thunder sounded in his heart
before the stillness; but to me the question
remained unanswered: Lord of the West and East,
Maker of earth and heaven and all the stars,
Are you accountable to your creation?

Sons of Eve

We were new as parents, Adam and I,
as all was new at dawning of our race.
In ignorance we had committed wrong
so serious that God must punish us
by taking from us our two well-grown sons.

I loved my second son, who bore the name
of Abel. From his early years he worked
among the flocks and herds. He knew their speech,
their simple needs and innocent desires;
and even with the wild ones of the forest
he held communion. Once with fearful heart
I saw a lion creeping toward my son
and would have run to save him, but before
my voice or feet could move, the lion sat
and licked my Abel's hand, doing no harm.

I loved as well his elder brother, Cain,
the leader in all things. His hands had skill
in coaxing earth to give her fairest flowers
and richest fruits with generosity.
A maker and a builder, he was glad
to help his brother build of polished stones
an altar for an offering to the Lord.

Cain had a choice of all things beautiful
to sacrifice; Abel had only one
most dearly prized possession, a ewe lamb
which from its birth had followed him. At morn
they romped together in the field; at night
it laid its trusting head against his feet.

Sons of Eve

Cain happily arranged his fruits and flowers
in glorious color on the altar stone.
Young Abel slew his lamb and offered God
his grief and pain, tears mingled with the blood.
I wept for him, his tenderness and courage.

Then something happened; they were strangely still,
as if they heard a Voice I could not hear
or saw a radiant light, though I was blind.
The moment passed, and Abel's face was changed
from pain to peace, from grief to ecstasy.
I turned to Cain, and I was shocked to see
his strange bewildered air, his angry look.

I know not what the Voice said to my sons,
a different word to each, but from that day
there was no peace between them. Every act,
each step of Abel's, only fed Cain's rage.
It seemed a madness; nothing I could do,
in all my love, could heal the deadly breach.
At last with heavy hand and furious strength
my Cain struck down my Abel. Both of them
were lost to me, in exile and in death.

For a long time their father and I despaired.
We never spoke of them, tried to forget
the grief of Abel and the shame of Cain.
He did his best to comfort me, but still
the tragic question echoed in both minds:
Is this the end? Is there to be no future,
God's sacred promise not to be fulfilled?

Our punishment endured; though sorrowing still
we held our faith in God's just grace. At last
we gained a measure of tranquility
and were rewarded with another son.
We named him Seth, and lavished on this boy
the whole accumulation of our love.
He grew and thrived; the promise was fulfilled.

I have a vision of my child, a man
taking his place in the ancestral line,
parent to child to parent; using earth
and earth's materials evermore to build
bodies to live and die, cities to raise
tall towers that crumble into desert sand,
nations to boast and conquer for a while
then wither, be absorbed and disappear.

Yet for a short time he was ours alone.
One day he raised his innocent eyes to mine
and asked, "Who are my brothers? Where are they?"
It almost stopped my heart. I tried to find,
as parents must, the words he'd understand,
to tell him what I scarcely comprehend
myself. Did I succeed in answering him?
I do not know; the mystery remains.
I wonder if this third son hears the Voice.
For him the meaning, his the task to come.
I who have eaten of the tree of death
resign the future to my unborn heirs.

Daughter of Lot

I, Amhara, with my sister, Dinah,
stood at the harem window looking down
on the white roofs of Sodom, where my father
maintained his office at the city gate;
for he was a judge, empowered to pass upon
entry and exit of all foreigners.
Our house stood on a little eminence
outside the wall. My father would not live
in the vile city, nor permit his daughters
to set foot in its streets. Even the concubines
must stay in the house. They were content to stay
for women led a sorry life in Sodom.

My sister Dinah came and stood with me.
"Look," she said, "our father is coming home.
Who are those strangers, one on either side,
who walk with him?" One of the concubines
peered over our shoulders and said mockingly
perhaps her lord was bringing home two husbands
found in the market place, to give his daughters.
I struck her and rebuked her insolence.
But Dinah looked at me; I knew her thought.
These men wore shining silk, and walked so nobly
They might indeed be princes from afar,
such men as Lot would choose to wed his daughters.
A noisy rabble followed them, closing in
as they approached the door; their cries became

Daughter of Lot

audible to us, asking for the two
fair strangers, that their vicious lust might work
its will on them. My father turned and shouted,
"Be off, you scum! Rather my virgin daughters
should fall into your hands, than these who claim
the sacred rite of hospitality."

They made to storm the door. One of the guests
stepped forward, holding up a hand wherein
the only weapon was a tiny spark
which broadened to a searing knife of flame
and struck the men of Sodom blind. Screaming,
groping, they reeled and staggered down the hill
back to their lair, and we were free of them.

There was a legend in the house of Terah,
our uncle, Abraham, had talked with angels;
and one who carried lightning in his palm
was surely more than human, more than prince.
"My daughters, Dinah, Amhara, greet our guests,"
our father said, and modestly we knelt,
in hopeful wonder.

                         But they had not come
to look on us, or speak to Lot of marriage.
Sent by the Lord, they came to give us warning.
The wicked cities, Sodom and Gomorrah,
within a day would be destroyed by fire.
Our household could be saved only by flight
before the break of dawn.

Daughter of Lot

                         My father called
the concubines and servants, bidding them
prepare to go with us. They only laughed
and murmured that the master had gone mad;
they would not go. My mother thought the same,
but she could not defy her lord's command.
We must leave quickly and on foot.

                           We dressed
in the coarse garb of servants, and put off
our dainty sandals for their heavy shoes.
We made small packs of necessary things
to bind upon our unaccustomed shoulders.
My mother would not change her silken robe
or carry any burden. We set forth,
on a dark path lighted only by a glow
that shone around the form of him who led.

We crossed the valley. On the opposite hill
Dinah said, "Let us stop for one last look."
But in a voice not to be disobeyed
our guardian spoke, "Move on, and look not back!"
My mother did not hear, or would not heed.
She ran ahead, leaped up on low rock
and turned her face for one last view of Sodom.
We saw a dreadful whiteness come upon her,
she became still as stone, one gasping word
frozen on her pale lips, and it was death.
My father touched her hand -- and it came off
and lay in his palm, a heap of stinging ash.
He cast it from him with a terrible cry

and reeled, and would have fallen but strong arms
supported him. "Move on, and look not back,"
they said again. Our faltering feet obeyed.
With downcast eyes we passed that grisly statue,
one handless arm half raised as in farewell.

The friendly guardians helped us to pursue
a weary way; how long, how far we traveled
I never knew. The one who walked with me
gave strength and courage, sometimes with a word
of tenderness, more often silently.
I knew that Dinah had a like support.
Lot walked alone; in body he was strong
but his shocked mind was clouded and bemused.
We reached a hidden valley where wild fruit
hung heavy, watered by a gentle stream.
I know not what the others saw or heard
for all my mind was centered on my guide,
who stood before me, calling me by name.
"Amhara, in all love I leave you now.
A lifetime lies between us, we shall meet
if you have strength to do what must be done
and bear what must be borne." I felt a kiss
glow on my forehead like a star. When tears
cleared from my eyes I saw we stood alone,
two desolate women and a man distraught.

The fertile valley was inhabited
by strange small hairy people, men and women
both shaggy as their goats, but peaceable.
They brought us food and offered us a cave.

Daughter of Lot

Lot, with his bearded face and simple mind,
they did not fear, but Dinah and myself
they held in awe for we were tall and smooth,
too strange to be desired. The little women
served us without a thought of jealousy.
And they were right; there was no fitting mate
among this uncouth tribe, nor anywhere
for women who had glimpsed angelic love.

We made a sort of life but ill-content
among this alien and inferior race.
Was it for this we had escaped the fire
to live forever barren, unfulfilled?

Harem reared, well versed in woman lore,
not all of it innocent, our ripe young bodies
cried out for motherhood. Deliberately
we laid our plan. With wine we made Lot drunk
beyond all sense, and in his drunken sleep,
dreaming perhaps of concubines, he lay
with each of us in turn, and we conceived.
Knowing how we had dared the wrath of God,
we had nine months to wonder what might come,
sons, daughters, monsters? We could only wait.

The little hairy women tended us
with skill; for Dinah and I were brought to bed
both in one day, and could not help each other.
If we had offended God, there was no curse;
our sons were healthy, perfect, beautiful.

Daughter of Lot

In the hour of blissful slumber which sometimes
comes to requite a woman after pain
I had a dream. My angel stood beside me.
Touching the child, he said, "His name is Moab.
He and his brother-cousin will be men
great in their time, leaders of two tribes."
As a scroll he held the future to my sight,
recurrent faces, now and then a name.
One far-off daughter turned to smile at me;
I heard the name of Ruth; and of her sons,
the poet kings, David and Solomon,
whose songs outlive their reign; and later on
there was a girl called Mary, then a light
so dazzling bright that I woke with a cry.
The baby Moab clutched at my flowing breast.
I lay at peace and pondered on these things.
The dream was true. We lived to see our sons
grow tall and wise, and travel far to build
strong tribes. We went with them and made a part
in all their work, doing what must be done.

Now I am old. My sister comes to me
only in sleep and always with a smile.
The faces of my dream, seen in the flesh,
have now grown dim, voices sound distantly.
I am brim full of memories, having room
for only one desire. My hand is held;
this lifetime lies behind me; I move on.

Sarah

Abram of Ur, my husband, talked with God.
I did not listen to their conversation
for I was Sa-ra-i, the beautiful,
whose chief concern it was to be admired,
adorned with jewels for my lord's delight,
cherished and shielded from all coarsening toil.
I could look forward to a life of ease
in well-known customs and familiar scenes.
Later, much later, with my beauty spent,
I might achieve fruition in my body
and be an honored matron in the tribe;
but Abram's God made havoc of my hopes.

> Now the Lord said unto Abram:
> Get thee out of thy country
> and from thy kindred
> and from thy father's house
> unto a land that I will show thee,
> and I will make of thee a great nation,
> and I will bless thee and make thy name great.

The voice spoke with such power and certainty
that Abram had no thought but to obey.
He undertook the careful preparation
to move his many flocks and herds, and all
the families dependent on his word.

The tedium of such a caravan,
timed to the footing of the slowest ox,
was almost unendurable to me,
accustomed as I was to luxury

Sarah

in all the pleasant comfort wealth can give.
Abram spared nothing to alleviate
the hardship of my journey. Four of the best
and brightest of the servants, bearing fans
and fragrant viands, walked beside the litter
in which I rode on cushions, canopied,
my bearers trained to move with gliding step
that I might not be shaken or disturbed.
And though within my heart I always longed
for the cool fountains and the courts of Ur
I made no loud complaint, but ever tried
to greet my husband with a cheerful face
and keep myself serene and beautiful.

We made our way into the land of Canaan
and were received without hostility;
for though the natives were barbarians
they knew of the great city in Chaldea
where wise men read the stars to prophesy.
They did not doubt that Abram had been led
to Canaan by a god. They let him choose
a dwelling place and build a sacred altar.

There came a year when famine smote the land
and we went south to Egypt where was food.
We were not young; my husband's beard was white
though he was strong, with all his manly powers.
But my famed beauty hardly seemed to change
with age. (I do not speak from vanity;
it was acknowledged as a fact by all.)
And only I knew of the single hair
among the curling masses on my head

that raised a signal of encroaching years.
Gladly I went to Egypt. There the art
and implements of beauty were well known.
I would employ their skill, and find a woman
to serve my body, keep it beautiful.

> It came to pass that Abram said unto Sarai:
> I know that thou art a fair woman to look upon;
> Therefore it shall come to pass,
> when the Egyptians shall see thee,
> that they shall say, This is his wife:
> and they will kill me, but they will save thee alive.
> Say, I pray thee, thou art my sister.

This was a hasty lie, and ill-conceived,
unworthy of the wisdom of my lord,
and I could see how it might lead to trouble:
but mine was not to argue. I obeyed
and called myself his sister, thinking too
it might be rather sweet to be desired
by an Egyptian prince. Let Abram deal
with this, if the occasion should arise.

We prospered well in Egypt and acquired
more wealth. They did not call us Canaanites
but knew from our good quality of life
that we were, as we claimed to be, Chaldeans.
High nobles sought us out, to talk with Abram
and look at me. I had but to return
the glance, however modestly, and know
the man was mine, if I so wished. Indeed
I was not false, or anything but chaste,
yet I did act my part with subtlety

Sarah

and some enjoyment. So, it came about
that a great princess took me to her house
so that her brother, as I later found,
conveniently might woo me for a wife.
Of course the truth came out, disastrously.
My angry suitor poured rebuke and scorn
on Abram for the clumsy stratagem.
"Is it your country's custom," cried the prince,
"to kill a man for his wife? I had thought better
of your Chaldean wisdom. Take your wealth
and get you back to Canaan whence you came.
You are not fit to live with honest folk."

We brought Egyptian servants back to Canaan.
My handmaid, Hagar, was a clever girl,
not fair of face, but graceful as a bird
and skilled in feminine lore, the artful use
of essences and lotions to preserve
a good appearance to an aging body.
Ten years in Canaan passed without event
save that the former promise was renewed
that all this land would be a heritage
of Abram's seed "like to the dust of earth
in numbers." But there had not been a child
conceived by me, now threescore years and ten.
The promise could not be fulfilled through me.
Who then but Hagar? She was wholly mine
to do my bidding. I commanded her
to lie with Abram and produce a son,
and quickly she conceived. I shed no tear,
for how could I be envious of a slave?

Sarah

Abram came in from walking in the field,
dusty and hot, and Hagar ran to fetch
cool water and a cloth to lave his feet:
It was a common service; she knew not
that I was watching. When she bent her head
to dry his foot, I saw her press a kiss
upon the instep; then I saw him smile;
reach forth his hand and lay it on her head.
I held my peace, but later when I found
my lord alone, I said, "Hagar must go.
I cannot tolerate her insolence.
She flaunts her pregnancy, to my reproach."
"But you — " he started to protest, and then
he caught my eye and changed his tone. "She is yours,"
he muttered, "Deal with her as you see fit."
And so I sent her forth, but she came back
saying an angel had appeared to her
with a command to give me full submission
and never to offend again by word
or glance or gesture. All this talk of angels
meant little to me, but I had missed her service.
I took her back and let her bear her child,
a healthy son, who was named Ishmael,
well loved by Ahram but ignored by me.

Three holy men appeared before my tent,
 greeted by Abram with such reverence
I knew they must be messengers of God.
While I prepared rich food to honor them
I listened as I could to what they said.
Our names were to be changed to Abraham
and Sarah; the strong promise was repeated

Sarah

of a great multitude in Abraham's line
and through a child of mine. I laughed aloud.
Husbands, angels, gods! all of them male;
what did they know of women? I was nearly
ninety years old; nature had drained me dry.
And so I laughed, until I was rebuked
and humbled, for the angel spoke the truth.

I was as awkward as a virgin bride
when Abraham came to me, but a son
was thus conceived and in due time was born.
A strange new life was mine, and such a love
as I had never known possessed my soul,
for all my world was centered on my son.
He grew in strength and beauty as the years,
like moments to the aged, swiftly passed.

My husband spoke to me of Isaac's marriage.
A sudden dreadful pain shot through my heart
till I was like to die; and every time
the matter was discussed the pain recurred
till Abraham was frightened, and forbore.

Now Isaac is thirty-seven years of age;
the time has come when he must bring a wife
to share his love and my authority.
Oh God of Abraham, be merciful
and let me die before I see that day.

Rebekah

We rested through the heat of afternoon.
My father, calling, roused me from my nap,
"Rebekah, time to fill the water jars."
I yawned and stretched, complained, "It's still too hot,"
but knew that I must be about my task.
My brother Laban would not be asleep
with all the servants busying themselves;
the daughter of the house must do her part.
I drew myself out of a pleasant dream
wherein a handsome prince had offered love.
I glanced at my young body, warm and ripe,
and took no shame to own that I was fair.
I donned my working robe and sturdy sandals
and took the water pots down to the well.

There I beheld a man, dusty with travel,
who had just left a passing caravan.
"Let down your pitcher and give me a drink,"
he begged. I drew cool water for the man
and for his camels. These poor homely beasts
are always thirsty, though they go for days
with groan and protest bearing heavy loads
across the scorching desert without drink.
He thanked me for my kindness, asked my name.
"Rebekah, daughter of Bethuel," I told him.
He raised his hands and said, "The Lord be praised!"
(I knew not why) and offered me a gift,
a bracelet of soft gold which I still wear
with pride. I led him to my father's house.

Rebekah

He was a trusted servant of our uncle
Abram, who had sent him here to seek
a wife for his son, Isaac, of his own
good family, unmixed with heathen blood.
This was an honor, for my father knew
that Isaac was of princely heritage:
but he would not send me against my will
to dwell in a far land. He said, "My child,
this is your home and you shall not be sent
away from it save by your own free choice.
This marriage to your cousin seems all good
but search your heart and let God be your guide."
I thought of my dream. A prince had offered love
and I rejoiced; surely this was a sign.
The gold band on my arm grew strangely warm,
I answered without question, "I will go."

Isaac was watching: when he saw the camels
approaching in the distance, he rushed forth
to meet the servant and to question him.
"Were you successful? Have you found my bride?
When may I go for her?" And though he was
forty years old, it was on his tongue to ask,
"And is she fair?" like any eager boy.
All this he told me later. At the time
surprise had silenced him. He had not thought
that I would come so quickly. Had I shown
unseemly forwardness, at first I wondered.
But when the veil dropped from my face
we looked into each other's eyes and were assured,
for there we found an instant recognition
as of old friendship lovingly renewed.

So we were married and for twenty years
we lived in peace and harmony. Our joy
was only marred in that we had no child.
And every month through all that score of years
I bled with disappointment, tried to cheer
myself with thought of Sarah, who had borne
Isaac at ninety, by a miracle.
It was small comfort. Isaac loved only me
and would not take another wife. "Trust God,"
he said, "There is a promise." So we waited
and were rewarded: First the flutter came
of a new life in me, the certainty,
the quickening, which grew into a struggle
as twins began their quarrel in my womb.

Never were brothers less alike. The first
to be born, whom we named Esau, was a child
of large and bony frame and hairy skin
and such a great consuming appetite
that all my milk was needed to sustain him.
He pined and sickened on all other food.
The other baby, Jacob, fair and smooth,
was far more dear to me. I often wept
to give both breasts to Esau, while the child
I loved lay sweetly smiling, satisfied
with milk of goat, having no need of me.

After the period of their infancy
the brothers grew, each in his different way.
Both learned the skills of husbandry, the care
of flocks and herds, as was our way of life.

Rebekah

But Esau was a hunter, ever seeking
wild food. He brought his father venison
and Isaac loved him fondly. Jacob dwelt
more in the tent, and often talked with me.
His youthful mind was tuned to hidden meaning
and subtle thought, and I rejoiced in this,
to find companionship in one so young.

A widening rift began to show itself
in our small family, for more and more
did Isaac come to lean on his first-born.
He had been powerful in his time, but age
was blinding him and turning his desires
toward trivial comforts of the appetite.
He said to Esau, "I would have you go
and bring me venison for a savory stew
such as I love, that with my strength renewed
I may give you the blessing that confirms
your right as eldest son." And Esau went.

It is no secret now how Jacob and I
conspired to seize such opportunity.
I dressed him in the clothes that smelled of Esau,
prepared a savory stew from flesh of kid
with skill to make it taste like venison,
and sent him to impersonate his twin,
taking advantage of my husband's blindness.
I had no thought for anyone but Jacob,
my son so dearly loved. The thing was done,
the blessing given, not to be revoked.

Great was the grief and loud the sad outcry
when they discovered they had been betrayed.
My husband did not long survive the shock;
he died without a word of blame for me.
Esau, too, in all his natural rage,
blamed only Jacob. "When the mourning days
are past," he said with cold determined fury,
"I will kill him." This word was brought to me.
I sent for Jacob and commanded him
to flee from danger to my brother's house
and bide there until Esau's wrath had cooled.

Isaac is dead and Jacob gone. I am left
alone with the unloved son whom I have wronged.
May Abraham's God grant pardon and contrive
some good to come from all this wickedness.

Leah

I, Leah, wife of Jacob, tell a tale
of fraud and trickery, of patient love
and long deferred revenge. There is no book
for any man to write which will record
the loves and sufferings of us who bore
their children, ruled their households, and sustained
and comforted their bodies in the night.
Pride keeps us silent; but my pride was gone
after the rapture of my wedding night,
broken and shattered with the rising sun,
when Jacob, eyes still closed, enfolded me
in his arms and whispered, "Rachel, my love, my wife."
And when I did not speak, because I dared not,
he looked into my face, the poor plain face
of Leah. For a moment he was stunned
with disbelief; then, seeing the foul trick
that had been played by Laban, the bride's veil,
the unaccustomed wine, the darkened chamber,
he leaped from bed, and naked as he was
rushed out into the day. I wept alone.

Jacob was not the man for helpless rage
to blur and dominate his mind for more
than a brief time. Long afterward I learned
of the strange contract he had forced on Laban,
this time with signature and witnesses.
My husband was to stay with me one week,
establishing my status as his wife,

Leah

then he could marry Rachel, and would serve
seven more years in payment; there was some
provision for a further recompense,
but this I was not told. There was no great feast
when they were wed. Rachel had her own tent
and Jacob slept with her when he so wished.

In the next years he seldom came to me,
but I was fertile and I bore four sons,
Reuben, the firstborn, Simeon, Levi, Judah,
in quick succession, earning some approval,
if not the love I longed for, while my sister,
so beautiful, so dearly bought, was barren.
She gave her handmaid, Bilhah, fair and strong,
to Jacob, that a child which should be born
on Rachel's knees, would so become her own.
By this arrangement Bilhah bore two sons.

Doubly neglected, I was sorely grieved.
I called my servant, Zilpah, and required
that she should serve my lord in the same way.
She wept bitterly, begging to refuse
the honor, for she loved a shepherd lad
and wished no child by any other man.
I felt some pity, for I too had loved,
but forced myself to disregard her tears.
"Your body is my property," I said,
"It is not yours to give, you know the law.
So dry your eyes, my dear, and do your duty."
Her children had three parents but no love.

Leah

When Rachel had been his wife for some three years
I learned the rest of Jacob's shrewdest bargain:
his share of all the increase of the flocks,
all calves and lambs that were "ring-straked and speckled"
and every kid born brown. Those were so many
that Laban stood to lose most of the young.
Jacob, his plan in mind, had used to breed
only the dark and speckled rams and bulls
and had set up beside the watering place
large spotted rods, where all the pregnant beasts
would drink the sight in as they took their water.
I counseled Zilpah not to wander near
these rods for Jacob would not care to have
his own progeny born ring-straked and speckled.

The day arrived when the long servitude
came to an end. Jacob was to depart
for Canaan. He prepared his herds and flocks
and many servants with their families,
his own four wives and their eleven sons;
for I had borne two more, and at long last
Rachel had blossomed into motherhood.
Her Joseph, the most beautiful of all,
was Jacob's pride and joy, in infancy
the petted darling of the families.

Laban and Jacob were both devious men
and did not trust each other, but they parted

Ring-straked: *Marked with circular stripes.*

Leah

courteously with the Mizpah covenant
bidding the Lord to keep watch between them
in absence, when they could not watch each other.

In his more prosperous days Laban had bought
three Moabitish gods to guard his tent,
with ugly faces but of purest gold.
These Rachel stole, and when she lay a-dying
after Benjamin's birth, while we were still
on our long journey to the land of Canaan,
confided to my care, a legacy
to her two sons, and I received the charge.
My sister died and our long rivalry
was ended. Jacob fastened his whole heart
on the two youngest sons, but there was room
for me to share his loss and mourn our dead.

The scribes may write the story of our travel,
of war, rapine and treachery, interspersed
with altars built and brothers reconciled.
Leave it to them; I play a woman's part,
aloof from war and worship and fierce jests.
The journey ended here at Bethlehem,
near the old family home. We settled down
where there was water and abundant food
and room for flocks to pasture far afield.
A passing caravan would sometimes stop
to rest the camels and take on supplies.

One merchant opened up his pack to show
a gorgeous coat, brought from the Orient,
embroidered in such colors as before

we did not know existed; and the lining
was rich and lovely as the outer part
with scarlet, purple, green and indigo.
The trader looked at Joseph, then sixteen,
tall, handsome as an angel, then he slipped
the coat on the young shoulders for display.
Jacob made him an offer, but he laughed,
"I daresay you are rich in sheep and cattle
but an Egyptian prince will give me gold
enough to comfort my declining years."
I saw the yearning in my husband's eyes
and went to fetch one of the three gods
Rachel had stolen and left in my charge.
The merchant said, "For two such images
I would sell the coat." Jacob was delighted
to make this princely present to his favorite.

But there were mutterings among the brothers
who had already been provoked by Joseph,
his youthful arrogance, the dreamer's tales
of his own greatness, which had long since ceased
to be amusing; now this latest sign
of doting preference brought them close to hate.
The brothers took the sheep up to the hills
for summer pasturage and there encamped.
When Jacob thought to send a messenger
to find out how they fared, young Joseph pled,
"Let me go, father. I would see the camp."
Permission granted, he set smartly forth
in foolish vanity wearing the fine coat
of many colors. He did not return.

Leah

Instead came Judah, carrying the garment
torn and stained with blood. It had been found
so Judah said, close to a wild beast's lair.

Then Jacob bowed his head and mourned again
as he had mourned for Rachel. I too wept
for I had loved the boy. When Judah saw
my grief, he pitied, and told me the truth:
that Joseph had been sold to slavery.
Should I tell Jacob? I had known years of hope
and disappointment, when with each new child
I thought I might have earned some real love.
Of these two miseries I had come to know
uncertain hope is worse than certain grief.
Better his father should think Joseph dead
than picture him beneath a slaver's whip.
So I kept silence, and I took the cloak,
mended the rent with careful stitchery,
washed out the stains and laid it in the chest
which held the legacy for Benjamin
now only one gold Moabitish idol.

Twelve years have passed. I have been stricken down
and have not long to live. Farewells are said,
ten older sons and little Benjamin,
for I have been mother to them all.
I know they do not wish to sadden me
with mention of the lost one, but the voice
of Joseph, dead or alive, speaks in my heart.

Lastly came Jacob. Kneeling by my couch,
he took my hand, whispering tenderly,
"Leah, my good and faithful wife." I felt
his tears upon my hand, a full reward.
I lie at ease, awaiting the great sleep.
The patient woman watching by my bed
has served me well, I give her one more task:
Zilpah, at last I am made beautiful;
bring the bright cloak and spread it over me.

David's First Wife

How beautiful he stood before the king,
stroking his harp, singing his shepherd song:
for after he had brought Goliath's head
and laid the gory trophy at Saul's feet
the king commanded music to cleanse the air.
My brother Jonathan and I, the princess,
Michal by name, listened and looked and loved
once and for all. We two were near of age
and so alike that in his beardless days
with an exchange of clothing we could pass
one for the other. Also in our hearts
and minds we were as one. When sudden love
for David overcame us both, there was
this difference, that Jonathan could go
and clasp him in his arms, while I must sit
serene, controlled, wearing my princess smile
rent with the first of many jealous pangs,
and wait for David to be brought to me.

King Saul was eloquent with words of praise
for the youth's valor, beauty, gift of song.
There were great promises of high preferment.
And he should marry -- here my heart stood still —
one of Saul's daughters; have a host of men
under his leadership. These were fair words
but in my father's voice I could detect
a note of fear and envy boding ill;
I silently prayed: Beloved, do not trust him.

David's First Wife

We did not know a demon had entered Saul
to foul his heart and dispossess his mind.
It came and went, each visit leaving him
moodier and more unpredictable.
Sometimes the charm of David's harp and voice
would drive it out, but then it would return
more violently. Once it threw a javelin
aimed at the singer's head, missing the mark
only because of the agility
wherewith he leaped aside, leaving the weapon
quivering embedded in the palace wall.

David and Jonathan, whose souls were knit
with love, in some strange way made room for me
to share their intimacy, and there were
some happy times when we were young together.
Of course I could not go with them to war,
and there was always fighting. The Philistines
saw us as the invaders, and themselves
as brave defenders of their Palestine,
its vineyards, its walled cities and their homes.
But when I mentioned this the young men laughed
and said the people of the Lord must fight,
exterminate the heathen, and regain
the heritage of Abraham. A woman
could not expect to understand such things.

Saul's demon throve on natural jealousy,
for the young singer was the people's hero
and could become a rival for the throne,
and every time the men went out to war
my father hoped that David would be killed.

David's First Wife

And several treacherous attempts were made
to take his life by covert means, leaving
the king appearing blameless; but the servants
were loyal more to Jonathan and me
than to their master, so his life was saved.

Belatedly remembering his promise
that David should become his son-in-law
in one of his less frequent kindly moods
the king published news of our betrothal.
The nation all rejoiced, all but one man,
Phal-ti-el, who had loved me long; his heart
was crushed. I pitied him, for he was good
and I could well have been content with him
if David had not shone into my life.

I look upon those days of happiness
as set apart from all the rest of time,
for they were brief. Wherever David went
on his campaigns, he found a willing woman.
I heard of Abigail, the generous,
who robbed her husband's larder to give aid
and comfort to the troops, and then remained
to be with David and to bear him sons.
He fathered many sons by various women
but not by me. I thought I was forgotten.

When Phal-ti-el became importunate
my father gave me to him, cancelling
my former marriage. I obeyed without
protest. My heart was numb and dry with grief.

David's First Wife

The long war lingered on; then one sad day
the message came that Saul and Jonathan
had died in battle, fighting side by side.
I mourned my dear-loved brother. There were tears
also for the father of my youth.
Phal-ti-el gave me comfort in this sorrow
and I was grateful for his tenderness.

David was king. The gentle shepherd lad,
the valiant youth, the singer of sweet songs,
the mighty warrior, hero of the people
was crowned and ruled in Hebron. He remembered
he had a wife called Michal, who was sister
to his loved Jonathan. He sent for me
Abner, the general, head of all the army,
with orders that I must return with him.
Phal-ti-el cried aloud, "Was it for this
I fought to make him king, and lose my all?"
He would have followed when the litter came
to bear me off, but with rebuke and threat
the general drove him back, and he went weeping.
We never met again. I did not know
why I was sent for. How had David changed?
Surely he could not love me still. And I?
There was no question there. The love that blazed
into a flame with my first sight of him
had never been extinguished, only hidden.
I did not look for happiness, to be
one of his women, but I must endure
whatever came with dignity and courage.

David's First Wife

When I came home to David's arms it seemed
as though I had never left them. All the years
that lay between us, all his other loves
were nothing now. There were no barriers.
I was to him another Jonathan
to share his inmost self; and he could speak
to me as to no other; this was joy.

He still made songs. It was his great delight
to hear a hundred golden voices pour
a hymn to God, in words that he had set
to noble music. Men came from afar
to join the choirs of Jerusalem,
and special skill with voice or instrument
assured their welcome. I had part in this,
for David pleased to bring me each new psalm
and hear it with my ears. At night sometimes
we lay till dawn, talking of many things.
If there was jealousy among the palace women
I neither knew nor cared; I was secure.

Then the Philistines returned the Ark.
I watched from a high window as my lord
King David capered in the street for joy,
his tunic flying up with every leap.
When he returned to bless our house I met him
and scolded him for loss of dignity,
thus to cavort before the maids. He laughed,
"I danced before the Lord; He knows my ways.
A man who trusts in God and in himself
may also trust his natural impulses
to do no wrong or no unseemly thing."

David's First Wife

I think that there were those who pitied me
because I bore no children, and indeed
I would have welcomed woman's usual gifts
but found rich happiness in what I had,
the generous overflow of a great mind.
It might be thought that in his settled years,
weighted with cares of state, highly endowed
with power and glory, poetry and song,
this noble king would find himself immune
to the base lusts and sudden madnesses
that do beset an ordinary man.

Then came Bathsheba. She was virtuous
and innocently mourned her husband's loss:
never believing, if she heard, the tale,
the ugly tale men whispered in the street,
that David had contrived Uriah's death.
I only knew he came no more to me
with a fresh song or a bright thought to share.
No doubt he was absorbed in his new wife,
but I think also that he feared to see
himself reflected in my knowing eyes.
Even his psalms were stale and repetitious,
devoid of their early fervor, praising God
as from afar, not daring to approach.
Later there was a prayer of penitence,
"Out of the depths have I cried to Thee, O Lord."

* * * * * * * *

Jonathan had been dead and David crowned
for forty years. Old age had crept upon us.
To me it brought a long review of life
in pictured memory, turning page by page.

David was stricken with a deadly chill
into his bones. Some of the fools around him
came bringing a plump young virgin to his bed
"to give him heart," they said. He faintly laughed
and sent her home with gifts, and turned his face
to the wall, bidding the world be gone.
The final hour was come. They let me in
to stand beside his bed and look my last.
I touched his hand; strangely a look of youth
came to his face. He whispered "Jonathan,"
then spoke no more, and Solomon was king.

Naomi the Weaver

I was a thread in a great tapestry,
but this I did not know when I was young,
thinking myself the weaver, the designer.
I was a woman vigorous and shrewd
but loving, and the careful plans I made
were all for those I loved, not for myself,
or so I thought. When drouth and famine came
I would not stay to see my children starve.
There was abundance in the heathen land
of Moab, and I resolutely brought
my family to live there. We could eat;
and when the famine ended could return
to Judah, where my infant sons when grown
would take good wives that I would choose for them
among our own, the people of the Lord.

But time flew by; the famine lingered on
in our home land. The heathen were not all
as bad as we had heard. They showed me kindness
when Elimelech died, who was my husband;
and where there's kindness surely Israel's God
has spread his hand, call it by any name.

Soon, too terribly soon, my sons were grown
and of an age to marry. I had tried
to rear them in the precepts of our faith
and had so far succeeded that they kept
the law of Moses. But the Moabite girls
were fair and gentle, many virtuous

Naomi the Weaver

according to their standards. When my sons
brought Ruth and Orpah home to live with us
I could not well refuse them. For a while
we lived in quiet family happiness.
I loved these daughters, for they learned our ways
and were in all things sweet and biddable.
There would be grandchildren to bless my age
and I would teach them; I was still the weaver,
the designer.

   Then the sudden knife death
cut through the warp. The strong young men were gone,
leaving three widows; mine was a double grief.
We could not stay there; one roof was too small
to cover so much sorrow. I would go
back to my country, where the drouth had ceased
and there was bread, not that it mattered much
whether I lived or died. But Ruth and Orpah
were young and beautiful; they must return
to their own people, and perhaps remarry.
They both agreed; and when the parting hour
was on us Orpah kissed me sad farewell,
but Ruth clung to me, and the words she spoke
a poet later made into a song:

> Entreat me not to leave thee
> or to return from following after thee,
> for whither thou goest I will go
> and where thou lodgest I will lodge.
> Thy people shall be my people and thy God my God.
> Where thou diest will I die
> and there will I be buried.

> The Lord do so to me and more also
> if aught but death part thee and me.

Ruth was no singer, but she spoke her heart.
The clinging arms, the gentle loving voice
were balm to my sore soul. I bade her come.
We joined a little caravan, and walked
beside the beast that bore our folded tent
and meager household gear; for the most part
moving in silence, busy with our thoughts.

We came to Judah in the harvest time
and pitched our tent among the very poor
who came to glean, according to the law
which grants the poor some standing and some rights.
I was too spent with travel to go out
on the first day, so Ruth went forth to glean
alone. She was assigned a place to work,
as it so happened, following the swath
of a most careful reaper, who let fall
few stalks of grain. Thus at the close of day
when every worker passed the harvest master
Ruth had poor showing for her weary labor.
Boaz, the master, saw the lovely girl
turn to go home, bearing her pitiful sheaf,
and spoke to the good reaper, bidding him
henceforth to be more liberal with his leavings.

Boaz was of my husband's distant kin.
We had no real claim on him, but I saw
that he had noticed Ruth. I counseled her,
for she was without guile, how to approach him.

Naomi the Weaver

This story, too, is written in a book
wherein the scribes keep record of our people,
for they were married and she bore him sons.
They gave me a home; I helped Ruth rear her children
and this was great happiness to me.

Now age has quieted my busy hands
and I can look upon four generations.
I see us all as threads in a design,
some bright with color, others of a shade
for necessary background, but each soul
resilient with its own will and purpose.
Some day, it may be, I will seek a prophet
and ask him to explain this mystery.

APPENDIX

PUBLICATION HISTORY AND OTHER INTERESTING DETAILS

1940
Not previously published.

A Happy Thought
Published in *A Square Inch of Space* (1974)

A Hope
Published in *A Square Inch of Space* (1974)

A Long View
Published in the Independent Journal (Marin County, California), "Marin Poets' Corner", April 27, 1963.

A Prayer
Published in *A Square Inch of Space* (1974)

A Simple Man
Published in *A Square Inch of Space* (1974) under the title "Sketch From Life"

A Small Adventure
Not previously published.

A Small Song
Published in *A Square Inch of Space* (1974)

A Song
Not previously published. Handwritten in Sibyl's Journal at the back of her Baby Book, probably prior to 1910.

A Sower
Published in *A Square Inch of Space* (1974) under the title "A Sower Went Forth To Sow"

A Square Inch of Space
Published in *A Square Inch of Space* (1974). Slightly different version entitled "Needlework" in June, 1972, Mu Phi Epsilon "Triangle"

A Whimper
Not previously published.

After a Thousand Years
Published in *A Square Inch of Space* (1974)

Aftermath
Not previously published.

Airless Night
Not previously published.

Almost a Memory
Not previously published.

Appendix

Always
Published in *A Square Inch of Space* (1974)

An Answer
Not previously published. Written in Sibyl's Journal at the back of her Baby Book, probably prior to 1910.

An Article of Furniture
Published in *A Square Inch of Space* (1974), Mu Phi Epsilon *Triangle* in March, 1954, and again in June, 1972.

An Unusual Honor
Not previously published. Noted as "first draft" November, 1978.

Antaeus
Published in *A Square Inch of Space* (1974)

Ants
Not previously published.

Apropos of Roses
Not previously published.

As It Might Happen
LA poetry award 1935 (exact details unknown). Published in *A Square Inch of Space* (1974)

Babel
Not previously published. Dated December, 1976.

Bell Team, The
Not previously published.

Berry Hill
Not previously published. Dated March, 1980.

Birth and the Pursuit of Happiness
Not previously published.

Body Speaks, The
Not previously published.

Bronze Chrysanthemums
Not previously published.

California Summer Song
Published in *A Square Inch of Space* (1974)

Call Me Buck
Published in *Mock Us Gently* (1978)

Cameos
Published in *A Square Inch of Space* (1974)

Cat in the Old Village Grocery
Not previously published.

Caterpillar, The
Not previously published.

Channel 5
Published in *Mock Us Gently* (1978)

Chess or Contract
Not previously published.

Civilized Rabbit, The
Published in *A Square Inch of Space* (1974)

Crusade Spirit, The
Not previously published. Dated 1974.

Dark Water
Not previously published.

Daughter of Lot
Not previously published. Written in the early 1970's as part of a series of poems about the women of the Bible. The story is in Genesis 19:1-38.

David's First Wife
Not previously published. Written in the early 1970's as part of a series of poems about the women of the Bible. The story is in Samuel Chapters 6, 18-22.

Dawn Stirrings
Published in *A Square Inch of Space* (1974)

Departure
Published in *A Square Inch of Space* (1974)

Dialog with a Strawberry
Published in *Mock Us Gently* (1978)

Don't Feed the Pigeons
Published in *Mock Us Gently* (1978)

Dream Children
Not previously published. It refers to an entry about a dream in Sibyl's Baby Book when she was about 2 years old.

Dream
Not previously published. Dated January 1975.

Dryads Curious
Published in *A Square Inch of Space* (1974)

Dryads
Not previously published.

Dust Thou Art
Not previously published.

Empty Chairs
Published in *A Square Inch of Space* (1974)

Eternal Joy, The
Not previously published.

Exit Line
Published in *A Square Inch of Space* (1974)

Fate and Love
Not previously published. Written in Sibyl's Journal at the back of her Baby Book, probably prior to 1910.

Felines
Published in *A Square Inch of Space* (1974) and in Mu Phi Epsilon "Triangle" (June, 1972).

Fern Fingers
Published in *A Square Inch of Space* (1974). Also noted as having been published in *Warp and Woof* (unknown date); copy not located.

Flattery Will Get You
Published in *Mock Us Gently* (1978)

Fondly Remembered
Published in *Mock Us Gently* (1978)

For Happiness
Published in *A Square Inch of Space* (1974)

Forbidden Fruit
Published as a "competitive poem" in *A Day in the Hills: A poetical competition of the Edwin Markham Chapter of the English Poetry Society* edited by Henry Meade Bland, privately printed, 1926.

Freedom
Not previously published.

Friends
Not previously published.

From a Car Window
Not previously published.

From California
Published in Independent Journal (San Rafael, CA), "Marin Poet's Corner", May 10, 1975.

Fugue by Wilhelm Friedmann Bach
Published in *A Square Inch of Space* (1974)

Fur Cup, The
Published in *A Square Inch of Space* (1974)

Fur Saucer, The
Published in *A Square Inch of Space* (1974)

Fur Spoon, The
Published in *A Square Inch of Space* (1974)

Appendix

Geography and Poetry
Published in unknown newspaper (probably near Lincoln, CA, ca 1899). Poem prefaced with "This is the way the sixth grade pupils of the Fruitvale school (Mr. Harley, teacher) prepare their geography lessons for easy memorizing:" The clipping was glued into Sibyl's Baby Book with a note in Sibyl's hand: "Written in collaboration with a friend of my own age at 11 years of age."

Ginkgo Tree, The
Published in *A Square Inch of Space* (1974)

Good News on the Radio
Not previously published.

Grandma Eschews Parsley
Not previously published.

Green Things
Published in *A Square Inch of Space* (1974)

Has All Been Said
Not previously published.

He Stirreth Up the People
Published in *A Square Inch of Space* (1974)

Heaven
Not previously published. Written in Sibyl's Journal at the back of her Baby Book, probably prior to 1910.

Her Picture
Not previously published.

Herself
Published in *A Square Inch of Space* (1974)

Hokku for Tears
Not previously published.

Hokku of Expectancy
Not previously published.

Hokku of Happiness
Not previously published.

Hokku of Pain
Not previously published.

Home-Coming
Published as a winning poem in *A Day in the Hills: A poetical competition of the Edwin Markham Chapter of the English Poetry Society* edited by Henry Meade Bland, privately printed, 1926.

Published in *A Square Inch of Space* (1974).

Also noted as having been published in "Anthology of California Poets" and Santa Ana Daily Register, August 10, 1955, but copies have not been located.

Houses
Published in *A Square Inch of Space* (1974)

I Am What I Am When I Am
Published in *A Square Inch of Space* (1974)

I Hate Dogs
Not previously published.

I See a Boy
Noted as having been published August 15, 1961; publication unknown.

I Warn You
Published in *A Day in the Hills: A poetical competition of the Edwin Markham Chapter of the English Poetry Society* edited by Henry Meade Bland, privately printed, 1926.

Published in *A Square Inch of Space* (1974).

I Was Privileged
Published in *Mock Us Gently* (1978). This poem recounts a woman passing on while Sibyl was playing Brahm's Lullaby. Sibyl said that she was very proud and honored to have been able to ease the woman's passing with her music.

If I Will
Published in *A Square Inch of Space* (1974). Another slightly different version entitled "Fragment", unpublished.

Publication Details

Immortality
Not previously published.

In a Garden
Published in *A Square Inch of Space* (1974). Clipping from a prior publication (date, publisher unknown) with author stated as "Sibyl Croly Hanchett" (so it was published prior to 1940 or so, when she remarried).

Incident in a Low Key
Published in *Mock Us Gently* (1978)

Incomplete
Published in *A Square Inch of Space* (1974)

Inconsistency
Not previously published. Written in Sibyl's Journal at the back of her Baby Book, probably prior to 1910.

Is That So
Not previously published. Dated October, 1978.

Jealous Doggy-Rel
Not previously published.

Jymn's Hymn
Not previously published.

Kind Souls
Not previously published.

Kings 1:1-4
Published in *A Square Inch of Space* (1974)

Knight Errant
Published in *A Square Inch of Space* (1974)

La Noche
Not previously published. Written in Sibyl's Journal at the back of her Baby Book, probably prior to 1910.

Leah
Not previously published. Written in the early 1970's as part of a series of poems about the women of the Bible. The story is in Genesis Chapters 29-35.

Looking Back
Not previously published

Machine Age, The
Published in *A Square Inch of Space* (1974)

Man in the Moon, The
Not previously published

Marc
Not previously published.

Martyr Complex
Not previously published.

Merry Christmas - Happy New Year
Not previously published. Dated December, 1976.

Mill Valley to Malibu
Not previously published. Written in the late 1970's.

Mock Us Gently
Published in *Mock Us Gently* (1978)

Moon Driven
Not previously published.

Moonin'
Published in *A Square Inch of Space* (1974)

Moving Day (Inventory)
Not previously published.

Music Critic
Published in *Mock Us Gently* (1978)

My Education (Hieronymus Bosch)
Not previously published.

Appendix

My Pearls
Not previously published. Written in Sibyl's Journal at the back of her Baby Book, probably prior to 1910.

My Town
Published in *A Square Inch of Space* (1974)

Naomi the Weaver
Not previously published. Written in the early 1970's as part of a series of poems about the women of the Bible. The story is in Ruth Chapters 1-4.

New England Ancestry
Published in *A Square Inch of Space* (1974)

New Orleans, 1960
Published in the Independent Journal (Marin County, California), "Marin Poets' Corner", November 26, 1960, under the title "One New Orleans Mother".

Published in *A Square Inch of Space* (1974).

New Year's Eve of 1905
Not previously published. Dated 1978.

No Candle Burning
Published in *A Square Inch of Space* (1974)

Nor the Alternative
Not previously published.

Office Secretary, The
Not previously published.

Old Friends
Published in the Independent Journal (Marin County, California), "Marin Poets' Corner", July 1, 1961.

Published in *A Square Inch of Space* (1974).

Old Rose
Not previously published. Dated November, 1978.

One Answer
Published in *Mock Us Gently* (1978)

One of Life's Moments
Published in *Mock Us Gently* (1978)

Only With Music
Published in *A Square Inch of Space* (1974)

Ordeal at Dawn
Not previously published.

Our Grandchildren
Published in *Mock Us Gently* (1978)

Overheard
Published in *Mock Us Gently* (1978)

Pastime
Published in *A Square Inch of Space* (1974)

Philosopher, The
Published in *A Square Inch of Space* (1974)

Piano, The
Not previously published. Written in Sibyl's Journal at the back of her Baby Book, probably prior to 1910.

Pippa Passes
Not previously published.

Place Names of Marin
Not previously published.

Poet Lovers
Not previously published.

Poet, The
Published in *A Square Inch of Space* (1974)

Prelude
Not previously published.

Privacy Achieved
Not previously published.

Quiet Repose
First poem, written at age 7 for her sister's wedding. Recorded by Sibyl's father in Sibyl's Baby Book.

Re-Verse

Not previously published.

Realism

Published in unknown newspaper, unknown date. Clipping pasted in Sibyl's Journal at the back of her Baby Book, probably prior to 1910.

Rebekah

Not previously published. Written in the early 1970's as part of a series of poems about the women of the Bible. The story is in Genesis 24:1-67.

Resistance

Not previously published.

Romance, Love

Not previously published.

Rude Words

Not previously published. Dated January, 1977.

Sarah

Not previously published. Written in the early 1970's as part of a series of poems about the women of the Bible. The story is in Genesis 16:1-16.

Schweitzer

Published in *A Square Inch of Space* (1974)

Self-Restraint in April

Published in *A Square Inch of Space* (1974)

Shh!

Published in the Mu Phi Epsilon "Triangle" (June, 1972).

Published in *A Square Inch of Space* (1974).

Shopworn

Not previously published.

Short Story

Not previously published.

Silence

Published in *A Square Inch of Space* (1974)

Sinner, The

Published in *Mock Us Gently* (1978)

Sons of Eve

Not previously published. Written in the early 1970's as part of a series of poems about the women of the Bible. The story is in Genesis 4:1-22.

Spring Scenario

Not previously published.

Squandered

Not previously published.

Stately Names of England

Not previously published.

Story of Cain as Told By His Wife, The

Not previously published. Written in the early 1970's as part of a series of poems about the women of the Bible. The story is in Genesis 4:1-22.

Suppliant, The

Published in *A Square Inch of Space* (1974). Also noted as published in *Warp and Woof*, but a copy has not been located.

Surrealist Trilogy

Published in *A Square Inch of Space* (1974)

Survival

Published in *A Square Inch of Space* (1974)

Teacher, The

Published as a competitive poem dedicated "To Doctor Bland" in *A Day in the Hills: A poetical competition of the Edwin Markham Chapter of the English Poetry Society* edited by Henry Meade Bland, privately printed, 1926. Published in *A Square Inch of Space* (1974)

Appendix

Tell the World
Not previously published. Dated June, 1980.

Terrible Words
Not previously published. Dated June, 1976.

Thirty Seven to Seventeen
Not previously published.

To a Fair Lad
Published in *A Square Inch of Space* (1974)

To a Greek Head
Published in the Anthology section of *A Day in the Hills: A poetical competition of the Edwin Markham Chapter of the English Poetry Society* edited by Henry Meade Bland, privately printed, 1926. To A.J.C.

To Art Eisler
Not previously published.

To M.D.
Not previously published.

To Sara Teasdale
Not previously published.

To the Father Tree
Not previously published.

Too Late Smart
Included in an article about Sibyl in the Mill Valley Record, July 31, 1974.

Too Short a Dream
Not previously published.

Truth
Not previously published.

Two Big Words
Published in *Mock Us Gently* (1978)

Two Loves
Not previously published. Written in Sibyl's Journal at the back of her Baby Book, probably prior to 1910.

Unexpressed
Not previously published.

Unfinished Story
Not previously published. Sibyl's fifth child, Alfred Robert, died of polio at the age of 3 months.

Unfit
Not previously published.

Unfriendly Skies
Not previously published. Dated December, 1976.

Valentine Verses
Not previously published. Written in Sibyl's Journal at the back of her Baby Book, dated Feb. 14, 1902 "Local hits on the school children and teacher." Apparently written by Sibyl for other children in the class.

Violet
Published in *Mock Us Gently* (1978)

Vision Before Choice
Published in *A Square Inch of Space* (1974)

We Entertained Royalty
Published in *Mock Us Gently* (1978)

Wheel Chair, The
Published in *Mock Us Gently* (1978)

When One Book Closes
Published in the ARE Journal, Volumes 5-6 (1970).

Published in *A Square Inch of Space* (1974).

Also included in an article about Sibyl, "Not just a 'Little Old Lady Poet'," published in the San Francisco Chronicle, March 8, 1979.

Whisper, The
Published in *Mock Us Gently* (1978)

Whither From Earth
Published in *A Square Inch of Space* (1974)

Wholesome Fun
Published in *A Square Inch of Space* (1974)

Why Bother
Noted as having been published in "C+M" (unknown publication), August 15, 1961.

Published in the Mu Phi epsilon "Triangle", June, 1972.

Published in *A Square Inch of Space* (1974).

You and I Were Young, Maggie
Published in *Mock Us Gently* (1978)

You Could Manage a Star
Published in *A Square Inch of Space* (1974) entitled "You Could Handle a Star"

Young Feet
Published in *A Square Inch of Space* (1974)

Young Hero
Not previously published. Dated November, 1980.

Youth
Published in *A Square Inch of Space* (1974)

INDEX BY TITLE

1940 89
A Happy Thought 84
A Hope.................176
A Long View 170
A Prayer................165
A Simple Man 63
A Small Adventure 29
A Small Song................108
A Song 55
A Sower 120
A Square Inch of Space.........106
A Whimper 47
After a Thousand Years..........130
Aftermath 56
Airless Night 84
Almost a Memory 42
Always 30
An Answer................114
An Article of Furniture 110
An Unusual Honor 141
Antaeus 125
Ants 136
Apropos of Roses.............164
As It Might Happen 171
Babel 119

Bell Team, The 86
Berry Hill.................. 90
Birth and the Pursuit of Happiness .16
Body Speaks, The 167
Bronze Chrysanthemums........175
California Summer Song 135
Call Me Buck 157
Cameos 165
Cat in the Old Village Grocery 131
Caterpillar, The 128
Channel 5.................152
Chess or Contract 57
Civilized Rabbit, The...........129
Crusade Spirit, The............107
Dark Water................. 53
Daughter of Lot 205
David's First Wife 231
Dawn Stirrings 82
Departure..................178
Dialog with a Strawberry.........154
Don't Feed the Pigeons 154
Dream Children 24
Dream 85
Dryads Curious 127
Dryads 126

Index by Title

Dust Thou Art 138
Empty Chairs 62
Eternal Joy, The 35
Exit Line 56
Fate and Love 100
Felines 132
Fern Fingers 124
Flattery Will Get You 146
Fondly Remembered 152
For Happiness 15
Forbidden Fruit 118
Freedom .130
Friends 21
From a Car Window 135
From California 101
Fugue by Wilhelm Friedmann Bach . 109
Fur Cup, The 186
Fur Saucer, The 187
Fur Spoon, The 188
Geography and Poetry 189
Ginkgo Tree, The 123
Good News on the Radio 91
Grandma Eschews Parsley 72
Green Things 125
Has All Been Said 83
He Stirreth Up the People 96
Heaven 177
Her Picture 62
Herself 61
Hokku for Tears 81
Hokku of Expectancy 80
Hokku of Happiness 80
Hokku of Pain 81
Home-Coming 71
Houses 169
I Am What I Am When I Am 167
I Hate Dogs 134
I See a Boy 25
I Warn You 54
I Was Privileged 151
If I Will 168
Immortality 163
In a Garden 124
Incident in a Low Key 155
Incomplete 58
Inconsistency 48
Is That So 64
Jealous Doggy-Rel 181
Jymn's Hymn 181
Kind Souls 15
Kings 1:1-4 116
Knight Errant 38
La Noche 140
Leah 223
Looking Back 30
Machine Age, The 37
Man in the Moon, The 46
Marc 69
Martyr Complex 64
Merry Christmas - Happy New Year 76
Mill Valley to Malibu 75
Mock Us Gently 145
Moon Driven 43
Moonin' .41
Moving Day (Inventory) 174
Music Critic 153
My Education (Hieronymus Bosch) 73
My Pearls 112
My Town 168

Index by Title

Naomi the Weaver 239	Short Story. 181
New England Ancestry 72	Silence 162
New Orleans, 1960. 93	Sinner, The 155
New Year's Eve of 1905 44	Sons of Eve. 201
No Candle Burning 53	Spring Scenario. 131
Nor the Alternative 31	Squandered 162
Office Secretary, The 66	Stately Names of England. 182
Old Friends 133	Story of Cain as Told By His Wife, The 195
Old Rose 166	Suppliant, The. 136
One Answer. 150	Surrealist Trilogy. 186
One of Life's Moments 147	Survival 123
Only With Music 32	Teacher, The 178
Ordeal at Dawn 36	Tell the World 105
Our Grandchildren 148	Terrible Words. 107
Overheard 145	Thirty Seven to Seventeen 33
Pastime 107	To a Fair Lad 19
Philosopher, The 105	To a Greek Head 49
Piano, The 98	To A.J.C. 65
Pippa Passes 185	To Art Eisler. 66
Place Names of Marin. 74	To M.D. 67
Poet Lovers 34	To Sara Teasdale 68
Poet, The 67	To the Father Tree. 128
Prelude. 139	Too Late Smart 105
Privacy Achieved 70	Too Short a Dream 18
Quiet Repose. 18	Truth 108
Re-Verse .184	Two Big Words 148
Realism 22	Two Loves 50
Rebekah .217	Unexpressed 52
Resistance 93	Unfinished Story. 79
Rude Words 71	Unfit. 94
Sarah 211	Unfriendly Skies 141
Schweitzer 92	Valentine Verses 190
Self-Restraint in April 137	Violet 156
Shh! 17	Vision Before Choice. 161
Shopworn. 54	

Index by Title

We Entertained Royalty..........158
Wheel Chair, The 149
When One Book Closes 164
Whisper, The..................153
Whither From Earth 97
Wholesome Fun 118
Why Bother 76
You and I Were Young, Maggie ...149
You Could Manage a Star 31
Young Feet................... 20
Young Hero..................184
Youth 20

www.ingramcontent.com/pod-product-compliance
Lightning Source LLC
Chambersburg PA
CBHW080534170426
43195CB00016B/2557